THE BEST OF
SAINSBURY'S
QUICK
COOKING

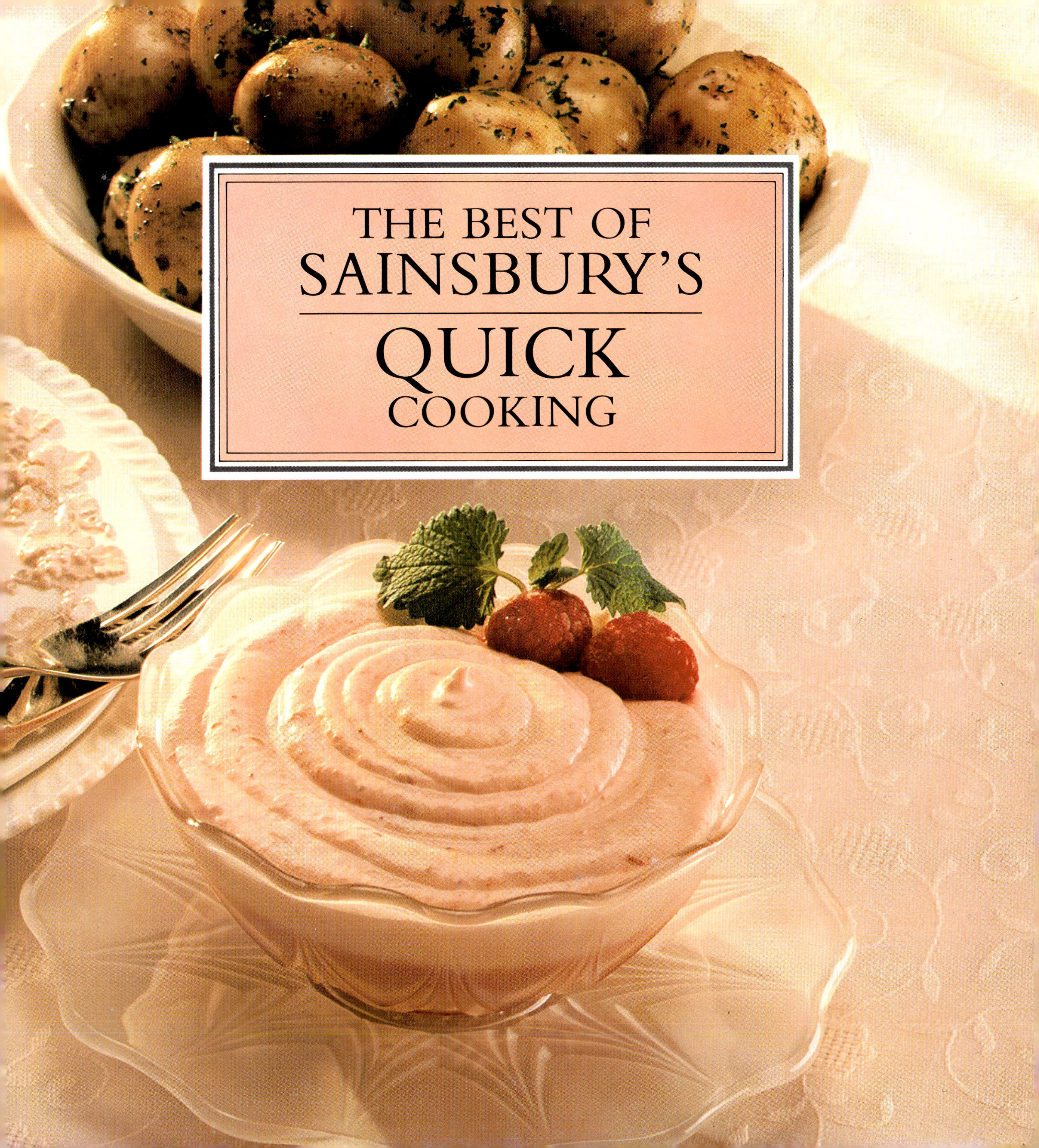
THE BEST OF
SAINSBURY'S
QUICK
COOKING

CONTENTS

CONTRIBUTORS

Main authors: Carol Bowen, Michelle Berriedale Johnson, Caroline Ellwood

Other contributing authors: Brian Binns, Margaret Fulton, Wendy Godfrey, Clare Gordon-Smith, Rita Greer, Carole Handslip, Gwyneth Loveday, Janice Murfitt, Rhona Newman, Mary Reynolds, Sue Ross, Margaret Weale

NOTES

Standard spoon measurements are used in all recipes
1 tablespoon = one 15 ml spoon
1 teaspoon = 5 ml spoon
All spoon measures are level.

Size 3 eggs should be used unless otherwise stated

Ovens should be preheated to the specified temperature

For all recipes, quantities are given in both metric and imperial measures. Follow either set but not a mixture of both, because they are not interchangeable.

Published exclusively for
J Sainsbury plc
Stamford House
Stamford Street
London SE1 9LL
by Cathay Books
Michelin House
81 Fulham Road
London SW3 6RB

First published 1987
Reprinted 1991

ISBN 0 86178 496 0

Produced by Mandarin Offset
Printed and bound in Hong Kong

INTRODUCTION

Endless hours slaving in a steaming hot kitchen don't necessarily mean perfectly cooked, wonderfully appetising and wholesome or healthy food. Indeed, often the opposite is true; a simply and speedily cooked dish presented imaginatively and elegantly can score many points over a fussily decorated, long-simmered dish of equal ingredients and cost.

All sorts of people need to prepare meals quickly for all sorts of reasons. There is the busy career-cook who has to concoct a meal at the end of a long and tiring day; the hard-pressed hostess who snatches odd moments throughout the day to prepare a dinner party; the housewife who asks guests to 'call anytime' and needs to conjure up an impromptu meal; and there are those who simply hate to spend time in the kitchen and slimmers who find it altogether too much of a temptation!

Luckily there are foods that might have been designed for quick-cooking – those tender cuts of meat and poultry like cutlets, steaks, breasts and liver that just need the flash of a flame; fish like salmon, sardines and prawns which need little more than a few minutes under the grill; rice; pasta, pulses and grains which respond to the quick-boiling treatment and countless vegetables, fruits and nuts that can be stir-fried to colourful, crunchy perfection. Although prime cuts are often more expensive than those which require long slow cooking, there is very little waste, and calculating portions is as easy as pie.

Quick cooking can also mean versatile cooking. Grilling, high temperature baking, frying, sautéeing, boiling, stir-frying and barbecuing being just a few of the many ways of cooking quickly. If cooking in a hurry is part of your way of life, then arm yourself with the very best quality battery of equipment for perfect long-term results. A good large wok, a heavy-based frying pan, a stay-clean grill and a sturdy barbecue will repay their cost in culinary dividends time and time again.

A well stocked storecupboard, refrigerator and freezer are also an enormous help to the successful busy cook. A wide selection of herbs, spices, essences, oils, dried fruits, nuts, vinegars, dried pastas, pulses and grains as well as fresh cheeses, savoury butters, dressings and dairy extras like yogurt, fromage frais and cream in all its guises will help you unlock the door to many new dishes. A good selection of frozen desserts will provide an instant and spectacular finish to the end of a short-notice dinner party.

Shortcut cooking shouldn't be jeopardized by slap-dash presentation. Whatever the occasion and however short the time, always aim to make dishes look attractive and appealing. A simple sprinkling of roughly chopped herbs, a scattering of nuts or croûtons, a well placed herb sprig, a lemon twist or a whirl of cream can make the world of difference. Garnishes and decorations only take seconds but they always show that thought and care have gone into the meal.

SOUPS AND STARTERS

A beautifully simple beginning to any meal may mean a velvety smooth soup, a hastily tossed but imaginatively concocted salad, a light-as-air fish mousse, a platter of crisp marinated vegetables or a colourful assembly of mixed antipasto.

Whatever the choice, the aim must be to stimulate the tastebuds for more treats to come, awakening rather than overwhelming the appetite for a main dish and a pudding or dessert.

Meal planning can be quite an art, but the secret of success lies in remembering to balance the relative weight of courses, hot dishes with cold ones and providing a variety of textures, flavours and colours. When a man-sized roast or hearty casserole is to be served, opt for a light starter such as Marinated Mushrooms, Eggs Mimosa or Mussels with Herb Butter, and when the main course or pudding are on the lighter side go for generous helpings of sustaining Provençal Vegetable Soup, New England Clam Chowder or a hearty Tuscan Bean Salad.

If time is at a premium before a special party, always try to prepare the soup or starter well ahead – many of the recipes in this section including soups, mousses, salads and marinated fish and vegetables can be made up to 48 hours in advance, or even longer if they are suitable for freezing. They can then be reheated to perfection, freshly tossed in a dressing, served with warm toast fingers or other accompaniments or given a special last minute garnish for same-day freshness. Such forward thinking gives the quick cook hostess more time to spend with her guests or to concentrate on the main course and dessert.

PROVENÇAL VEGETABLE SOUP

250 g (8 oz) courgettes, chopped
125 g (4 oz) leeks, chopped
500 g (1 lb) tomatoes, skinned and chopped
175 g (6 oz) carrots, chopped
500 g (1 lb) onions, chopped
250 g (8 oz) young runner beans
250 g (8 oz) French beans
250 g (8 oz) shelled broad beans
1.2 litres (2 pints) chicken stock
salt and pepper
125 g (4 oz) short-cut macaroni
50 g (2 oz) grated Parmesan cheese
PESTO:
4 cloves garlic
12 basil sprigs
4 tablespoons olive oil

Put all the vegetables into a large pan. Add the chicken stock, and season to taste with salt and pepper. Bring to the boil, cover and simmer for 15 minutes. Add the macaroni and cook for 10 to 12 minutes.

Meanwhile, make the pesto. Put the garlic and basil into a mortar and pound to a paste. Add the oil, drop by drop. Remove the soup from the heat and slowly stir in the pesto.

Ladle into a tureen or individual bowls, sprinkle with Parmesan cheese and serve immediately.

Serves 6

NOTE: When fresh basil is unobtainable, omit the pesto and add 2 cloves crushed garlic and 1 tablespoon chopped parsley to the soup, with the stock. Alternatively buy pesto ready-made from supermarkets and delicatessens.

MACKEREL IN WHITE WINE

300 ml (½ pint) dry white wine
150 ml (¼ pint) water
1 onion, sliced
1 fennel sprig
strip of lemon rind
6–7 peppercorns
2 bay leaves
salt
2 large mackerel, boned
2 teaspoons French mustard
2 tablespoons chopped parsley
fennel leaves to garnish

Put the wine, water, onion, fennel, lemon rind, peppercorns, bay leaves and a pinch of salt into a pan. Bring to the boil and simmer for 10 minutes. Cool, then strain.

Poach the mackerel in this liquid for 10 to 15 minutes. Cool, then strain, reserving half the stock. Arrange the fish on a serving dish.

Mix the reserved stock with the mustard and spoon over the fish. Sprinkle with parsley. Chill before serving, garnished with fennel.

Serves 4

MARINATED MUSHROOMS

3 tablespoons olive oil
4 shallots or small onions, peeled and chopped
4 tomatoes, skinned and chopped
4 peppercorns, crushed
6 coriander seeds
1 bay leaf
1 thyme sprig
salt
500 g (1 lb) button mushrooms
4 tablespoons dry white wine
2 tablespoons tomato purée
chopped parsley to garnish

Heat the oil in a pan, add the shallots or onions and fry until soft. Add the tomatoes, peppercorns, coriander seeds, herbs, and salt to taste. Stir in the mushrooms and wine, cover and simmer for 10 minutes.

Transfer the mushrooms to a serving dish. Discard the herbs. Bring the cooking liquor to the boil and boil for 5 minutes until well reduced. Add the tomato purée and spoon over the mushrooms. Sprinkle with parsley and chill before serving.

Serves 4

LEFT: *Provençal Vegetable Soup*
RIGHT: *Cream of Watercress Soup; Salade Niçoise*

CREAM OF WATERCRESS SOUP

40 g (1½ oz) butter
2 onions, chopped
350 g (12 oz) watercress
40 g (1½ oz) plain flour
1.2 litres (2 pints) chicken stock
salt and pepper
2 egg yolks
1 × 142 ml (5 fl oz) carton double cream
watercress sprigs to garnish

Melt the butter in a pan, add the onions and cook until soft, but not browned. Add the watercress and cook for 5 minutes until softened. Stir in the flour and cook for 2 minutes. Gradually stir in the chicken stock, bring to the boil and cook for 5 minutes. Season to taste with salt and pepper.

Sieve or work in an electric blender until smooth. Return to the pan.

Beat the egg yolks and cream together, then gradually add 300 ml (½ pint) of the hot soup, stirring constantly. Return to the pan and cook for 1 to 2 minutes; do not boil.

Pour into a tureen and garnish with watercress.

Serves 6

SALADE NIÇOISE

½ crisp lettuce
3 hard-boiled eggs
1 × 397 g (14 oz) can artichoke hearts, drained
1 × 198 g (7 oz) can tuna steak, drained
1 × 50 g (1¾ oz) can anchovy fillets
250 g (8 oz) tomatoes, skinned and quartered
125 g (4 oz) cooked French beans
8–10 black olives, stoned
1–2 teaspoons capers
1 tablespoon chopped parsley

DRESSING:

2 tablespoons lemon juice
4 tablespoons olive oil
1 clove garlic, crushed
pinch of sugar
salt and pepper
scant ½ teaspoon French mustard

Line a serving bowl with the lettuce.

Arrange all the salad ingredients in the prepared bowl.

Put the dressing ingredients in a screw-topped jar and shake well. Pour over the salad, toss well and serve immediately.

Serves 4 to 6

ANTIPASTO ALLA CASALINGA

2 green peppers
3 tablespoons olive oil
2 teaspoons wine vinegar
salt and pepper
4 tomatoes, sliced
few thinly sliced onion rings
1 × 198 g (7 oz) can tuna steak, drained and flaked
2 × 120 g (4 oz) cans sardines in oil, drained
2 tablespoons Mayonnaise (see page 21)

Place the peppers under a preheated hot grill until the skin is charred and blistered, turning frequently. Cut in half and rinse under cold water to remove the skin and seeds. Drain well and slice finely. Mix with 2 tablespoons of the oil, the vinegar and a little salt. Leave in the refrigerator until required.

Season the tomato slices with salt and pepper to taste and sprinkle with the remaining oil. Arrange the pepper slices in a large serving dish and top with the tomatoes. Scatter the onion rings over the top.

Pile the tuna in the centre and surround with the sardines. Serve with the Mayonnaise.

Serves 4

MUSSELS WITH HERB BUTTER

2.25 kg (5 lb) or 5 pints fresh mussels, scrubbed clean
2 glasses dry white wine
2 cloves garlic
6 parsley sprigs, chopped
6 basil sprigs, chopped (optional)
50 g (2 oz) butter, softened
2 tablespoons grated Parmesan cheese
basil or parsley sprigs to garnish

Discard any mussels that are open. Put the closed mussels into a pan, pour over the wine and bring to the boil. Cook until the shells have opened, discarding any that do not open. Strain the liquor through muslin. Crush the garlic in a mortar, add the herbs and pound. Add the butter and cheese; pound to a smooth paste.

Discard the empty half shell from each mussel. Spread the remaining mussel shell with the herb butter and arrange the shells on individual ovenproof dishes. Moisten with a little of the strained liquor.

Brown under a preheated hot grill. Serve at once, garnished with basil or parsley.

Serves 4

ANTIPASTI MISTI

3 tomatoes, sliced
3 tablespoons olive oil
1 teaspoon chopped basil or spring onion tops
salt and pepper
1 teaspoon lemon juice
1 clove garlic, crushed
1 fennel bulb, cut into strips
6 slices Italian salami
6 slices garlic sausage
50 g (2 oz) black olives, drained
2 hard-boiled eggs, quartered
basil or parsley sprigs to garnish

Arrange the tomatoes at one end of a large oval dish and sprinkle with 1 tablespoon of the oil, the basil or spring onion tops, and salt and pepper to taste.

Mix the remaining oil with the lemon juice, garlic, and salt and pepper to taste. Add the fennel and toss well. Pile at the other end of the dish.

Arrange the salami and garlic sausage in the middle of the dish. Top with the olives and surround with the eggs. Garnish with basil or parsley.

Serves 4

CHEESE NOODLES IN CHICKEN BROTH

1.2 litres (2 pints) chicken stock
1 egg, beaten
2 teaspoons plain flour
25 g (1 oz) grated Parmesan cheese
25 g (1 oz) dry white breadcrumbs
15 g ($\frac{1}{2}$ oz) butter, softened
pepper
grated nutmeg

Bring the chicken stock to the boil in a large pan.

Put the egg, flour, cheese, breadcrumbs and butter in a bowl. Add pepper and nutmeg to taste and work to a firm paste.

Press through a metal colander directly into the boiling broth. Simmer until the noodles rise to the surface, about 2 minutes.

Pour into individual soup bowls and serve immediately, with extra Parmesan cheese.

Serves 4 to 6

COURGETTE SOUP

40 g ($1\frac{1}{2}$ oz) butter
1 onion, sliced
500 g (1 lb) courgettes, thinly sliced
1.2 litres (2 pints) water
$1\frac{1}{2}$ chicken stock cubes
2 eggs
2 tablespoons grated Parmesan cheese
1 tablespoon chopped basil or parsley
salt and pepper
crostini (see below) or croûtons to garnish

Melt the butter in a saucepan, add the onion and fry gently for 5 minutes. Add the courgettes and fry, stirring frequently, for 5 to 10 minutes. Add the water and stock cubes, bring to the boil, cover and simmer for 20 minutes.

Purée in an electric blender or rub through a sieve. Return to the saucepan and bring to the boil.

Beat the eggs, cheese and herbs together in a warmed soup tureen, then slowly beat in the boiling soup. Check the seasoning, and pour into individual soup bowls. Top with *crostini* or croûtons and serve immediately.

Serves 4 to 6

CROSTINI: Cut round bread rolls into 5 mm ($\frac{1}{4}$ inch) thick slices and toast one side. Spread the untoasted side with butter, sprinkle thickly with grated cheese and place under a preheated hot grill until golden and bubbling.

LEFT: *Mussels with Herb Butter*
RIGHT: *Cheese Noodles in Chicken Broth; Courgette Soup; Minestra di Frittata*

MINESTRA DI FRITTATA

1.2 litres (2 pints) chicken stock
2 eggs
1 tablespoon plain flour
4 tablespoons milk
salt and pepper
a little oil
25 g (1 oz) grated Parmesan cheese
chopped parsley to garnish

Bring the chicken stock to the boil in a large pan.

Beat the eggs with the flour, milk and a little salt and pepper.

Lightly oil a large frying pan and place over high heat. When very hot, pour in the batter and cook for about 1 minute until set. Turn out, roll up and cut into thin strips. Add to the boiling broth with the cheese.

Serve immediately, sprinkled with parsley

Serves 4 to 6

Mushroom and Prawn Salad

PARMA HAM WITH MELON

4 slices Parma ham, or raw smoked ham
1 sweet ripe melon, chilled, quartered and deseeded
pepper

Drape the slices of ham over the melon. Serve with freshly ground black pepper.

Serves 4

DRESSED ARTICHOKE HEARTS

1 clove garlic, crushed
1 tablespoon lemon juice
4 tablespoons olive oil
salt and pepper
1 bay leaf
16 cooked fresh, or canned, artichoke hearts
1 tablespoon chopped parsley to garnish

Beat together the garlic, lemon juice, oil, and salt and pepper to taste in a bowl. Add the bay leaf and artichoke hearts and stir gently. Cover and chill for about 2 hours, stirring occasionally. Discard the bay leaf.

Divide the artichokes between individual dishes, spoon over the dressing and sprinkle with parsley.

Serves 4

MUSHROOM AND PRAWN SALAD

6 tablespoons olive oil
2 tablespoons lemon juice
pepper
1 clove garlic
350 g (12 oz) button mushrooms, thinly sliced
½ teaspoon salt
1 tablespoon chopped parsley
175 g (6 oz) peeled prawns

Beat the oil, lemon juice and a little pepper together in a mixing bowl. Add the garlic and mushrooms and stir gently. Cover and chill for at least 1 hour.

Just before serving, remove the garlic and stir in the salt and parsley. Transfer to a serving dish and top with prawns.

Serves 4

NOTE: Very fresh mushrooms and good olive oil are essential for this recipe.

EGGS WITH TUNA MAYONNAISE

200 ml (⅓ pint) Mayonnaise (see page 21)
1 × 99 g (3½ oz) can tuna steak
7 anchovy fillets
1 tablespoon lemon juice
4 hard-boiled eggs, halved lengthways
few capers
parsley sprigs to garnish

Put the Mayonnaise into an electric blender, add the tuna steak, 3 of the anchovy fillets and the lemon juice and work until smooth. If necessary, thin to a coating consistency by adding a little cold water.

Arrange the eggs, cut side down, on individual dishes. Cut the remaining anchovy fillets in half lengthways and curl one strip on top of each egg half. Sprinkle with capers and garnish with parsley. Put the Mayonnaise into a bowl and serve separately.

Serves 4

CREAM OF SWEETCORN SOUP

40 g ($1\frac{1}{2}$ oz) butter
1 onion, chopped
2 potatoes, diced
25 g (1 oz) plain flour
900 ml ($1\frac{1}{2}$ pints) milk
1 bay leaf
salt and white pepper
2 × 326 g ($11\frac{1}{2}$ oz) cans sweetcorn, drained
2 tablespoons double cream
crumbled fried bacon to garnish

Melt the butter in a pan, add the onion and cook for 5 minutes, without browning. Add the potatoes and cook for a further 2 minutes.

Stir in the flour, then gradually add the milk, stirring constantly. Bring to the boil, add the bay leaf and salt and pepper to taste. Add half the sweetcorn, cover and simmer for 15 to 20 minutes. Discard the bay leaf and cool slightly.

Sieve or work in an electric blender until smooth. Return to the pan, add the remaining sweetcorn and heat through.

Stir in the cream, sprinkle over the bacon and serve immediately.

Serves 4 to 6

CREAM OF CARROT SOUP

2 × 397 g (14 oz) cans carrots
2 onions, chopped
50 g (2 oz) butter
50 g (2 oz) fresh white breadcrumbs
600 ml (1 pint) milk
salt and pepper
chopped parsley to garnish

Put the carrots, with their juice, the onions, butter and breadcrumbs into a saucepan. Add the milk and bring to the boil. Cover and simmer for 5 minutes.

Rub through a sieve or work in an electric blender until smooth. Add salt and pepper to taste.

Reheat gently before serving, garnished with parsley.

Serves 4 to 6

POTAGE VERT

2 bunches of watercress
1 bunch of spring onions, chopped
250 g (8 oz) spinach
1 rosemary sprig
1 thyme sprig
4 tablespoons chopped parsley
600 ml (1 pint) chicken stock
salt and pepper
$1\frac{1}{2}$ teaspoons cornflour
120 ml (4 fl oz) double cream
squeeze of lemon juice
lemon slices to garnish

Put the watercress, spring onions and spinach into a large pan. Add the herbs and pour over the stock. Season with salt and pepper to taste. Bring to the boil, cover and simmer for 20 minutes. Cool slightly.

Sieve or work in an electric blender until smooth. Return to the pan and heat through.

Blend the cornflour with the cream, stir into the soup and bring to simmering point. Cook gently, stirring constantly, until thickened. Stir in the lemon juice.

Serve immediately, garnished with lemon slices.

Serves 4 to 6

Potage Vert

EGGS WITH PIQUANT MAYONNAISE

- *6 tablespoons thick Mayonnaise*
- *1 tablespoon lemon juice*
- *½ clove garlic, crushed*
- *2 tablespoons chopped parsley*
- *1 tablespoon chopped tarragon*
- *1 tablespoon chopped basil*
- *2 tablespoons capers*
- *2 × 50 g (1¾ oz) cans anchovy fillets, drained*
- *pepper*
- *1 head of frisé*
- *6 hard-boiled eggs, halved lengthways*

Put the Mayonnaise and lemon juice into a bowl. Mix in the garlic, herbs and 1 tablespoon capers. Chop half the anchovy fillets very finely and add to the Mayonnaise. Season with pepper to taste.

Place the frisé leaves on individual serving plates and arrange the eggs on top, cut side down. Spoon the herb Mayonnaise over and arrange the remaining anchovy fillets in a lattice pattern over each egg. Top with the remaining capers.

Serve chilled.

Serves 6

TOMATOES WITH FRESH HERBS

- *4 tablespoons chopped parsley*
- *2 tablespoons chopped basil*
- *2 tablespoons chopped tarragon*
- *2 tablespoons finely chopped onion*
- *2 spring onions, finely chopped*
- *1 clove garlic, crushed*
- *6 tablespoons olive or walnut oil*
- *3 tablespoons wine vinegar*
- *1 teaspoon clear honey*
- *salt and pepper*
- *8 large ripe tomatoes*

Mix the herbs, onions and garlic together, then gradually add the oil, vinegar and honey to form a thick sauce. Season well with salt and pepper.

Skin and slice the tomatoes. Arrange a layer on a serving platter and spoon over some dressing. Put another layer of tomatoes on top and spoon over more dressing. Continue with these layers until all the ingredients are used. Cover and chill for 30 minutes.

Serves 4 to 6

TUSCAN BEAN SALAD

- *1 × 425 g (15 oz) can cannellini beans, drained*
- *1 × 425 g (15 oz) can green beans or broad beans, drained*
- *1 small onion, thinly sliced*
- *6 tablespoons olive oil*
- *25 g (1 oz) black olives, stoned*
- *1 tablespoon chopped parsley*
- *1 tablespoon chopped oregano*
- *1 × 198 g (7 oz) can tuna steak, drained and flaked*
- *salt and pepper*
- *2 radicchio or chicory heads*

Mix the beans together in a bowl. Stir in the onion, oil, olives and herbs. Add the tuna to the salad. Toss well and season with salt and pepper to taste.

Arrange the radicchio leaves or chicory on a serving platter. Spoon the bean salad on top. Cover and chill until required.

Serves 4 to 6

ASPARAGUS GRATINÉE

4 slices wholemeal bread, toasted and buttered
1 × 340 g (12 oz) can asparagus spears, drained
50 g (2 oz) Cheddar cheese, grated
pepper

Arrange the toast in a shallow flameproof dish. Divide the asparagus spears equally between the toast slices and sprinkle with the cheese.

Place under a preheated hot grill for about 4 minutes, until the cheese has melted and is lightly browned. Sprinkle with pepper to taste and serve immediately.

Serves 4

ARTICHOKE HEART AND BACON SALAD

2 × 397 g (14 oz) cans artichoke hearts, drained
4 tablespoons French Dressing (see page 15)
50 g (2 oz) lean thick bacon rashers, cut into strips

Toss the artichoke hearts in the French Dressing and arrange in a serving dish.

Place a frying pan over moderate heat, add the bacon and fry in its own fat until crisp.

Sprinkle the bacon over the salad. Serve immediately.

Serves 4

FRENCH DRESSING

175 ml (6 fl oz) olive oil
4 tablespoons wine vinegar
1 teaspoon French mustard
1 clove garlic, crushed
1 teaspoon clear honey
salt and pepper

Put all the ingredients into a screw-topped jar, adding salt and pepper to taste. Shake well to blend before serving.

Makes 250 ml (8 fl oz)

LEFT: *Eggs with Piquant Mayonnaise; Tomatoes with Fresh Herbs; Tuscan Bean Salad*
RIGHT: *Eggs Mimosa*

EGGS MIMOSA

4 hard-boiled eggs, halved lengthways
1 × 42 g (1½ oz) can lumpfish caviar
6–8 tablespoons Mayonnaise (see page 21)
1 small lettuce to garnish

Remove the egg yolks and arrange the whites in a serving dish. Fill the egg white hollows with the caviar.

Rub the yolks through a sieve and spoon over the caviar, reserving 1 tablespoon for garnish.

Spoon the Mayonnaise over the eggs, covering them completely.

Garnish with the reserved egg yolk and lettuce. Serve with thin slices of brown bread.

Serves 4

VARIATION: Replace the caviar with 125 g (4 oz) lumpfish cod's roe, 150 g (5 oz) natural low-fat yogurt and the juice of 1 lemon. Mash these ingredients together, adding salt and pepper to taste, and use to fill the egg whites.

HONEYDEW MELON SALAD

500 g (1 lb) tomatoes
1 ripe honeydew melon, skinned
1 cucumber
4 tablespoons olive oil
2 tablespoons lemon juice
1 tablespoon chopped tarragon
1 tablespoon chopped parsley
1 tablespoon chopped chives
salt and pepper
few lettuce leaves

Set aside a few tomato slices for garnish. Skin and chop the remainder, discarding the seeds. Dice the melon and cucumber. Combine the melon, cucumber and tomatoes in a bowl.

Blend together the oil, lemon juice, herbs, and salt and pepper to taste. Spoon over the salad and mix well. Cover and chill for 2 to 3 hours. Arrange the lettuce in a bowl and pile the salad on top. Garnish with the tomato slices to serve.

Serves 6

CITRUS AND CHICORY SALAD

3 oranges, peeled and divided into segments
2 limes or 1 grapefruit, divided into segments
4 heads of chicory, sliced into rings
4 tablespoons olive oil
2 tablespoons lemon juice
1 teaspoon French mustard
salt and pepper
2 teaspoons chopped parsley
few lettuce leaves
lime or orange slices to garnish

Discard all the pith from the fruit and add to the chicory.

Blend the oil, lemon juice and mustard together. Season with salt and pepper to taste and stir in the parsley. Pour over the salad and toss well.

Arrange the lettuce in a salad bowl and pile the salad on top. Garnish with lemon or orange slices to serve.

Serves 4

ROSE SALAD

½ frisé or 2 radicchio
2 × 177 g (6 oz) cans crabmeat, drained and flaked
150 g (5 oz) peeled prawns
juice of ½ lemon
125 g (4 oz) tomatoes, skinned, seeded and chopped
few cooked whole prawns to garnish

DRESSING:

150 ml (¼ pint) Mayonnaise (see page 21)
2 teaspoons tomato purée
1 clove garlic, crushed
1 teaspoon chopped parsley
1 teaspoon chopped chives
salt and pepper

Mix all the dressing ingredients together, seasoning with salt and pepper to taste; cover and set aside.

Arrange the frisé or radicchio around the edge of individual plates or bowls. Mix together the crabmeat, prawns and lemon juice, and season well with salt and pepper. Stir in the tomatoes.

Spoon the mixture into the centre of the plates and pour over the dressing. Garnish with the whole prawns.

Serves 4 to 6

AVOCADO WITH PEARS AND BLACK OLIVES

2 avocados
2 tablespoons lemon juice
6 large black olives, halved and stoned
1½ tablespoons Mayonnaise (see page 21)
1 × 212 g (7½ oz) can pear quarters, drained and diced
salt and pepper

Halve and stone the avocados and rub with a little of the lemon juice to prevent discoloration.

Set aside 4 olive halves for garnish; chop the remainder.

Mix the Mayonnaise and remaining lemon juice together in a bowl. Add the pears, chopped olives, and salt and pepper to taste.

Pile the mixture into the avocado halves. Garnish each portion with an olive half.

Serves 4

Rose Salad

MUSSEL ANTIPASTO

1.75 kg (4 lb) or 4 pints fresh mussels, scrubbed clean
300 ml ($\frac{1}{2}$ pint) boiling water
3 cloves garlic, crushed
2 teaspoons grated lemon rind
3 tablespoons chopped parsley
1 basil sprig, chopped
2 thyme sprigs, chopped
40 g ($1\frac{1}{2}$ oz) fresh white breadcrumbs
5 tablespoons olive oil
parsley sprigs to garnish

Discard any mussels that are open. Put the closed mussels into a pan with the boiling water. Cook until the shells have opened, discarding any that do not open. Drain.

Discard the empty half shell from each mussel. Arrange the mussels in their half shells in a large shallow flameproof dish, or individual dishes.

Mix the garlic, lemon rind, herbs and breadcrumbs together and sprinkle over the mussels. Spoon over the oil and place under a preheated moderate grill for 5 to 7 minutes, until pale golden; do not overcook or the mussels will become tough.

Serve immediately garnished with parsley.

Serves 4 to 6

BROAD BEANS À LA GRECQUE

2 tablespoons oil
1 clove garlic, thinly sliced
1 onion, finely chopped
500 g (1 lb) shelled broad beans
8 tomatoes, skinned, seeded and chopped
2 tablespoons dry white wine
1 tablespoon chopped parsley
1 bay leaf
salt and pepper

Heat the oil in a pan, add the garlic and onion and fry for 4 to 5 minutes, without browning.

Stir in the broad beans and toss well to coat in the oil. Add the remaining ingredients, with salt and pepper to taste. Bring to the boil, cover and simmer for 15 minutes or until the beans are tender. Remove the bay leaf and leave to cool.

Serve chilled, with brown bread.

Serves 4

NOTE: Frozen broad beans can be used: cook the tomato mixture for 10 minutes before adding them.

POTTED KIPPERS

2 pairs smoked kippers
150 g (5 oz) unsalted butter
grated rind and juice of $\frac{1}{2}$ lemon
pepper
1 × 142 ml (5 fl oz) carton double cream, lightly whipped
25 g (1 oz) concentrated butter or butter, clarified (see below)
few lemon slices

Dot the kippers with half the unsalted butter. Cook under a preheated moderate grill for 3 to 4 minutes on each side, basting occasionally.

Cool slightly, then remove the skin and bones. Place the flesh in a blender or food processor with the remaining unsalted butter and blend until smooth. Stir in the rind and lemon juice, and pepper to taste. Fold in the cream and transfer to a serving dish.

Spoon over the concentrated butter and chill in the refrigerator until set.

Garnish with lemon slices and serve with crusty bread and lettuce.

Serves 4 to 6

TO CLARIFY BUTTER: Melt, allow to settle, then strain through muslin. Concentrated butter is butter which has been clarified. It is now available in supermarkets and delicatessens.

Broad Beans à la Grecque

NEW ENGLAND CLAM CHOWDER

50 g (2 oz) butter
2 spring onions, chopped
40 g ($1\frac{1}{2}$ oz) plain flour
pinch of chilli powder
salt and pepper
600 ml (1 pint) fish stock
1 × 175 g (6 oz) can clams
125 g (4 oz) frozen peeled prawns, thawed
1 × 198 g (7 oz) can sweetcorn, drained
2 potatoes, cubed
1 × 142 ml (5 fl oz) carton soured cream
chopped parsley

Melt the butter in a pan, add the spring onions and fry until softened. Stir in the flour, chilli powder, and salt and pepper to taste and cook for 1 minute. Gradually add the stock and bring to the boil. Add the clams, prawns, sweetcorn and potatoes and simmer for 15 minutes, or until the potatoes are soft but still hold their shape.

Stir in the soured cream. Sprinkle with the parsley to serve.

Serves 4

CUCUMBER AND PRAWN SOUP

1 large cucumber
salt and pepper
2 × 150 g (5 oz) cartons natural low-fat yogurt
6 tablespoons lemon juice
250 ml (8 fl oz) single cream
2 tablespoons chopped chives
125 g (4 oz) shelled prawns

Grate the unpeeled cucumber into a bowl and sprinkle lightly with salt. Leave for 15 minutes.

Mix the yogurt, lemon juice and cream together and add to the cucumber. Stir in the chives, prawns and salt and pepper to taste.

Chill the soup for at least 1 hour before serving.

Serves 4

PRAWNS AND SCALLOPS IN GARLIC

25 g (1 oz) butter
2 tablespoons oil
2 cloves garlic, crushed
250 g (8 oz) peeled prawns
8 shelled scallops, halved
2 tablespoons chopped parsley
juice of $\frac{1}{2}$ lemon

Heat the butter and oil in a frying pan, add the garlic and fry for 2 minutes. Add the prawns and scallops and cook quickly for 2 minutes, or until the scallops are tender; take care not to overcook or they will become tough.

Stir in the parsley and lemon juice and serve immediately, with crusty bread.

Serves 4 to 6

Prawns and Scallops in Garlic

ASPARAGUS AND CRAB MOUSSE

1 × 340 g (12 oz) can asparagus spears, drained with liquid reserved
1 × 177 g (6 oz) can crabmeat, drained with liquid reserved
150 ml (¼ pint) fish or chicken stock (approximately)
25 g (1 oz) butter
25 g (1 oz) plain flour
15 g (½ oz) gelatine
3 tablespoons dry white wine
300 ml (½ pint) Mayonnaise (see right)
1 × 142 ml (5 fl oz) carton double cream, lightly whipped
lemon slices or whole prawns to garnish

Combine the liquid from the asparagus and crabmeat and add sufficient stock to make 300 ml (½ pint).

Melt the butter in a pan, stir in the flour and cook for 1 minute. Stir in the stock, bring to the boil and simmer, stirring, for 2 minutes. Roughly chop the asparagus and flake the crabmeat. Fold into the sauce.

Dissolve the gelatine in the wine over low heat, then stir into the asparagus mixture. Fold in the Mayonnaise and cream. Spoon the mixture into an 18 cm (7 inch) round tin or mould and chill until set.

Turn out onto a serving dish and garnish with lemon slices or whole prawns.

Serves 6 to 8

SMOKED TROUT MOUSSE

3 smoked trout
300 ml (½ pint) dry white wine
2 teaspoons finely chopped onion
½ clove garlic, crushed
1 parsley sprig
2 tarragon sprigs
1 thyme sprig
2 bay leaves
salt and pepper
1 × 284 ml (½ pint) carton soured cream
TO GARNISH:
lemon or lime slices
parsley sprigs

Place the trout in a pan with the wine, onion, garlic, herbs, and salt and pepper to taste. Cover and cook gently for 10 minutes. Lift the fish from the pan, reserving the cooking liquor. Discard the skin and bones; place the fish in an electric blender.

Boil the cooking liquor until reduced by one-third, then strain into the blender and work to a purée. Turn into a bowl and fold in the cream. Cover and chill until required.

Spoon into individual dishes and garnish with lemon or lime slices and parsley.

Serves 4–6

CHEDDAR AND PRAWN MOUSSE

2 eggs, separated
125 g (4 oz) matured Cheddar cheese, finely grated
1 tablespoon grated Parmesan cheese
2 teaspoons English mustard
chilli powder
grated nutmeg
salt
1 × 284 ml (½ pint) carton double cream
50 g (2 oz) peeled prawns, chopped
TO GARNISH:
whole prawns (optional)
lemon slices

Beat the egg yolks until pale in colour. Mix in the cheeses, mustard and chilli powder, nutmeg and salt to taste.

Whip the cream until it just holds its shape. Fold into the cheese mixture with the prawns. Whisk the egg whites until stiff, then fold into the mixture.

Spoon into 4 ramekin dishes and chill until required.

Serve garnished with prawns, if using, and lemon slices.

Serves 4

Cheddar and Prawn Mousse; Smoked Trout Mousse

PRAWN TARTLETS

1 × 215 g (7½ oz) packet frozen wholewheat shortcrust pastry, thawed
dill leaves to garnish
FILLING:
3 tablespoons Mayonnaise (see below)
3 tablespoons soured cream
1 tablespoon tomato ketchup
½ teaspoon Tabasco sauce
1 teaspoon chilli powder
2 tablespoons chopped chives
salt and pepper
175 g (6 oz) peeled prawns
7.5 cm (3 inch) piece cucumber, diced
2 tomatoes, skinned and chopped
2 hard-boiled eggs, chopped

Roll out the pastry on a floured surface to a 5 mm (¼ inch) thickness. Using a 7.5 cm (3 inch) fluted cutter, cut out 24 circles and use to line bun trays. Prick the pastry well and 'bake blind' in a preheated moderate oven, 180°C (350°F), Gas Mark 4, for 10 to 15 minutes, until firm. Cool on a wire rack.

Make the filling: mix together the Mayonnaise, soured cream, tomato ketchup, Tabasco, chilli powder, chives, and salt and pepper to taste. Add the remaining ingredients and stir well to mix. Check the seasoning.

Spoon the mixture into the cooked pastry cases. Arrange on a serving dish and garnish with dill leaves to serve.

Makes 24

MAYONNAISE

2 large egg yolks (Size 1 or 2)
1 teaspoon salt
2–3 teaspoons lemon juice
200 ml (⅓ pint) olive oil

Put the egg yolks into a small basin, add the salt and 1 teaspoon of the lemon juice and mix thoroughly. Add the oil drop by drop, stirring constantly, until the sauce becomes thick and shiny. Add the rest of the oil in a thin stream, stirring constantly. Add lemon juice to taste.

Makes about 300 ml (½ pint)

NOTE: It is essential that all the ingredients are at room temperature before you begin.

SCALLOP AND PRAWN BROCHETTES

150 ml (¼ pint) dry white wine
1 tablespoon raspberry vinegar
1 tablespoon chopped dill
½ teaspoon salt
12 large shelled scallops
1½–2 cucumbers, peeled and cut into 1 cm (½ inch) slices
8 Mediterranean prawns
15 g (½ oz) butter, melted
TO GARNISH:
tomato quarters
basil leaves

Put the wine, vinegar, dill and salt into a large pan, bring to simmering point and add the scallops and cucumber. Simmer for 1 to 2 minutes, then remove with a slotted spoon; reserve the cooking liquid.

Place a prawn at one end of 4 long kebab skewers, arrange the cucumber and scallops alternately on the skewers, then add another prawn.

Brush with the butter and cook under a preheated high grill, or on a barbecue, for about 3 minutes on each side, basting frequently with the reserved cooking liquid.

Arrange the brochettes on a warmed serving dish. Garnish with tomato and basil and serve with Tomato Sauce (see page 75).

Serves 4

Scallop and Prawn Brochettes

HUSS SALAD

500 g (1 lb) huss fillets, skinned
300 ml (½ pint) dry white wine or water
1 onion, roughly chopped
1 bay leaf
salt and pepper
500 g (1 lb) new potatoes, boiled and halved
½ cucumber, diced
1 × 250 g (8 oz) jar pickled sweet baby beetroot, drained and cubed
2 tablespoons capers
DRESSING:
150 ml (¼ pint) fromage frais
juice of ½ lemon
2 tablespoons chopped chives
1 tablespoon chopped chervil

Place the fish, wine or water, onion, bay leaf, and salt and pepper to taste in a pan and simmer for 10 to 15 minutes or until the fish flakes easily. Drain, cool and cube the fish.

Place in a large bowl with the potatoes, cucumber, beetroot and capers.

Mix the dressing ingredients together, with salt and pepper to taste, pour over the salad and mix well.

Serves 4

SMOKED EEL MOUSSE

350 g (12 oz) smoked eel, skinned, boned and flaked
125 g (4 oz) cottage cheese
1 × 142 ml (5 fl oz) carton soured cream
2 teaspoons grated lemon rind
1 tablespoon lemon juice
2 tablespoons chopped parsley
salt and pepper
TO GARNISH:
frisé leaves
cucumber slices

Put the eel into an electric blender or food processor, add the remaining ingredients, with salt and pepper to taste, and work until smooth. Transfer to a bowl and chill until required.

Spoon the mousse onto individual serving plates. Garnish with frisé and cucumber to serve.

Serves 4

SCAMPI AND AVOCADO SALAD

1 tablespoon olive oil
salt and pepper
250 g (8 oz) scampi
1 avocado
2 oranges, peeled and divided into segments
2 small heads of chicory, separated into leaves
DRESSING:
2 tablespoons olive oil
3 tablespoons orange juice
2 tablespoons lemon juice
1 tablespoon chopped chervil
1 teaspoon chopped chives

Heat the oil in a frying pan and sprinkle in a little salt and pepper. Add the scampi and sauté for 3 to 5 minutes, until white in appearance. Remove with a slotted spoon; reserve the oil for the dressing.

Halve, stone, peel and thinly slice the avocado. Arrange with the oranges and chicory on individual serving plates, with the scampi.

Put the dressing ingredients in a screw-top jar. Add the reserved oil, and salt and pepper to taste and shake well. Pour over the salads and serve.

Alternatively, chop all the salad ingredients, place in a serving bowl, pour over the dressing and toss well.

Serves 4

NOTE: If you want to serve the salad as a main course, increase the scampi to 500 g (1 lb).

KIWI AND TROUT SALAD

175 g (6 oz) smoked trout, skinned and filleted
2 dessert apples, cored and chopped
1 kiwi fruit, sliced
50 g (2 oz) flaked almonds, toasted
2 tablespoons soured cream
1 teaspoon lemon juice
2 tablespoons chopped mint
pepper
4 mint sprigs to garnish

Flake the fish into bite-sized pieces and put into a bowl.

Add the apples to the fish with the kiwi fruit, almonds, soured cream, lemon juice, chopped mint, and pepper to taste.

Mix well, divide between 4 serving plates and garnish with a mint sprig.

Serves 4

NOTE: If you want to serve this as a main course, double the ingredients.

Huss Salad; Scampi and Avocado Salad; Kiwi and Trout Salad

CREAMED MUSHROOMS ON TOAST

50 g (2 oz) butter
1 small onion, finely chopped
juice of 1 lemon
250 g (8 oz) button mushrooms, sliced
4 teaspoons cornflour
350 ml (12 fl oz) single cream
2 teaspoons curry paste
salt and pepper
4 slices wholemeal bread, toasted and buttered
chopped parsley to garnish

Melt the butter in a frying pan, add the onion and fry gently until soft. Add the lemon juice and mushrooms and fry gently for 3 minutes.

Stir in the cornflour and cook, stirring, for 2 minutes. Gradually add the cream and cook gently, without boiling, until thickened. Add the curry paste with salt and pepper to taste.

Divide the mixture between the hot toast slices. Garnish with parsley and serve immediately.

Serves 4

ROE-STUFFED BAKED TOMATOES

40 g ($1\frac{1}{2}$ oz) butter
1 small onion, finely chopped
50 g (2 oz) fresh white breadcrumbs
1 × 99 g ($3\frac{1}{2}$ oz) can smoked cod's roe
grated rind of $\frac{1}{2}$ lemon
salt and pepper
chilli powder
4 large tomatoes, halved, seeded and drained
2–3 tablespoons dry white wine
black olives to garnish

Melt 25 g (1 oz) of the butter in a frying pan, add the onion and fry until soft. Add the breadcrumbs and fry until golden. Keep 4 teaspoons of the mixture on one side.

Break up the cod's roe and stir into the breadcrumb mixture with the lemon rind. Season with salt, pepper and chilli powder to taste.

Fill the tomato halves with the cod's roe mixture. Spoon the wine over the filling. Sprinkle with the reserved breadcrumb mixture and dot with the remaining butter.

Cook in a preheated moderate oven, 180°C (350°F), Gas Mark 4, for 15 to 20 minutes until the tomatoes are just tender. Serve hot, garnished with olives.

Serves 4

Creamed Mushrooms on Toast; Roe-Stuffed Baked Tomatoes

SPINACH AND CREAM CHEESE PÂTÉ

1 × 227 g (8 oz) carton cream cheese
125 g (4 oz) frozen chopped spinach, thawed
few drops of Tabasco sauce
juice of ½ lemon
grated nutmeg
salt and pepper
4 lemon twists to garnish

Beat the cream cheese until soft. Drain the spinach thoroughly, then gradually add to the cream cheese, beating constantly.

Add the Tabasco, lemon juice and nutmeg, salt and pepper to taste. Continue beating until the pâté is thoroughly blended. Spoon into individual dishes and chill well.

Garnish each portion with a lemon twist. Serve with buttered wholemeal toast.

Serves 4

NOTE: Cooked fresh, or canned spinach may be used.

SARDINE EGGS

4 hard-boiled eggs, halved lengthways
1 × 120 g (4 oz) can sardines in oil, drained and chopped
1 tablespoon fresh white breadcrumbs
2 tablespoons Mayonnaise
1 tablespoon lemon juice
salt and pepper
chopped parsley to garnish

Remove the yolks from the eggs and mash them, then mix with the sardines, breadcrumbs, Mayonnaise and lemon juice. Season with salt and pepper to taste and beat until thoroughly blended. Pile the mixture into the egg white halves.

Garnish with parsley and serve with buttered wholemeal bread.

Serves 4

GARLIC BREAD

This popular accompaniment can be stored in the freezer for 1 week. Mash together 150 g (5 oz) butter, ¼ teaspoon salt and 3 crushed garlic cloves. Cut 2 French loaves into 5 cm (2 inch) slices, spread on both sides with garlic butter, reshape the loaves and wrap in foil. Heat from frozen, still wrapped, for 30 minutes in a preheated moderately hot oven, 200°C (400°F), Gas Mark 6 and serve immediately.

CHICKEN AND WALNUT PÂTÉ

175 g (6 oz) liver sausage
1 clove garlic, crushed
3 tablespoons medium sherry
125 g (4 oz) cooked chicken, chopped
50 g (2 oz) walnuts, roughly chopped
pepper
parsley sprigs to garnish

Mash the liver sausage thoroughly with the garlic and sherry until smooth.

Add the chicken, walnuts and pepper to taste. Spoon into individual dishes and garnish with parsley.

Serve with buttered wholemeal toast.

Serves 4

FRENCH BREAD PIZZAS

1 French loaf, halved lengthways

BASE:
1 × 64 g (2¼ oz) can tomato purée
1–2 teaspoons dried mixed herbs
1–2 cloves garlic, crushed (optional)

TOPPING:
4 tomatoes, sliced
125 g (4 oz) salami
8 rashers streaky bacon, derinded
2 tablespoons capers
125 g (4 oz) Gruyère cheese, grated

(Picture, page 6)

Spread the cut surfaces of the bread with the tomato purée. Sprinkle with the herbs and the garlic, if using.

Arrange the sliced tomatoes and salami on each piece of French bread. Lay the bacon on top, sprinkle with the capers and top with the cheese.

Cut each piece of bread into four. Place on lightly oiled baking sheets and bake in a preheated moderately hot oven, 200°C (400°F), Gas Mark 6, for 15 minutes. Serve hot.

Serves 4 to 8

NOTE: Topping ingredients can be varied according to taste.

VEGETABLE AND SALAD DISHES

Quick vegetable dishes needn't be mournful mouthfuls of plainly boiled vegetables as this chapter will amply illustrate. With a little extra thought, and just a little more time, you can enjoy colourful steamed or boiled assemblies, jacket-baked surprises, pan hot fritters and stir-fry vegetable sizzles of year-round vegetable goodness.

Many of the recipes in this chapter are delicious accompaniments to meat and poultry roasts, succulent fish dishes and pasta or rice offerings, but some will also provide main meal alternatives when a vegetarian-style option is required. Dishes like Potato and Cheese Pie, Vegetable Crumble and Spanish Eggs are hearty enough to satisfy man-sized appetites without the need for meat.

If a salad is the order of the day then you can feast upon an imaginative selection of side and main course ideas. They range from simple dishes like Carrot and Raisin Salad, Beetroot and Orange Salad and Date and Nut Salad to sophisticated and elegant treats such as Palm Heart and Avocado Vinaigrette, Potato and Sorrel Salad or Frisé and Gruyère Salad.

Salads are not simply for the summer. With their clever combinations of root, leaf, onion, fruit and nut ingredients, our salads are designed for year-round eating. Opt for a delicious Cabbage Salad with Peanut Dressing, Kidney Bean Salad and Piquant Winter Salad during the cold winter months, leaving Baby Tomatoes with Avocado Dressing, Chicken Liver and Spinach Salad and Italian Mixed Salad for warmer days when leafy salad vegetables are at their cheapest and best.

CORN FRITTERS

1 × 326 g (11½ oz) can sweetcorn, drained
2 teaspoons soft brown sugar
3 eggs, beaten
50 g (2 oz) butter, melted
4 tablespoons grated Parmesan cheese
salt and pepper
oil for deep-frying
watercress sprigs to garnish

Put the sweetcorn into a bowl. Add the sugar, eggs, butter, cheese and salt and pepper to taste. Mix thoroughly.

Heat the oil in a deep-fat fryer to 180°C (350°F). Drop tablespoonfuls of the corn mixture into the hot oil and fry for about 4 minutes, until crisp and golden.

Remove with a slotted spoon, drain on kitchen paper and serve warm, garnished with watercress.

Serves 4

VEGETABLE CRUMBLE

1 cauliflower, broken into florets
salt
2 tablespoons oil
4 tablespoons wholewheat flour
350 ml (12 fl oz) milk
1 × 326 g (11½ oz) can sweetcorn, drained
2 tablespoons chopped parsley
125 g (4 oz) matured Cheddar cheese, grated

TOPPING:

50 g (2 oz) wholewheat flour
25 g (1 oz) margarine
25 g (1 oz) porridge oats
25 g (1 oz) chopped almonds

Cook the cauliflower in boiling salted water for 5 minutes. Drain, reserving the water.

Heat the oil in the same pan and stir in the flour. Remove from the heat, add the milk, stirring until blended. Add 150 ml (¼ pint) of the reserved cooking liquid, bring to the boil and cook for 3 minutes, until thickened. Stir in the sweetcorn, parsley and half the cheese. Gently fold in the cauliflower and turn into a 1.5 litre (3 pint) ovenproof dish.

For the topping, put the flour into a bowl and rub in the margarine until the mixture resembles fine breadcrumbs. Add the oats, almonds and remaining cheese. Sprinkle over the vegetable mixture and bake in a pre-heated moderately hot oven, 190°C (375°F), Gas Mark 5, for 30 minutes, until golden brown and crisp.

Serves 4

BAKED ONIONS

4 large or 8 medium onions, unpeeled
salt and pepper
chopped parsley to garnish

Cut a small piece off the root end of each onion. Cut off the tops and make 4 vertical slits through the skin from the top to the middle of each onion.

Place on a baking sheet and cook in a preheated moderate oven, 180°C (350°F), Gas Mark 4, for 30 to 45 minutes, depending on the size of the onions, until the centres are tender.

Remove the skins from the onions. Season with salt and pepper to taste and garnish with parsley. Serve hot.

Serves 4

SPANISH EGGS

4 tablespoons oil
2 slices stale bread, cubed
2 large potatoes, diced
1 onion, chopped
125 g (4 oz) bacon, derinded and chopped
50 g (2 oz) French beans, cut into 5 cm (2 inch) lengths
6 tomatoes, skinned, seeded and chopped
2 courgettes, thinly sliced
8 thin slices garlic sausage, diced
4 eggs
1 tablespoon chopped parsley to garnish

Heat the oil in a large frying pan, add the bread cubes and fry until browned. Remove and drain on kitchen paper.

Add the potatoes to the pan, toss in the oil and cook for 15 minutes, until browned on all sides. Add the onion and bacon and cook for 2 minutes. Stir in the beans, tomatoes and courgettes and cook for 5 to 7 minutes. Stir in the garlic sausage.

Transfer to a large shallow ovenproof dish and make 4 hollows in the mixture with the back of a spoon; break an egg into each. Bake in a preheated moderate oven, 180°C (350°F), Gas Mark 4, for 12 minutes. Sprinkle over the fried bread and return to the oven for 3 minutes.

Sprinkle with the parsley and serve immediately.

Serves 4

CRISPY CORN BAKE

25 g (1 oz) plain flour
2 eggs, beaten
25 g (1 oz) soft brown sugar
25 g (1 oz) butter, melted
6 tablespoons milk
salt and pepper
2 × 326 g (11½ oz) cans sweetcorn, drained
1 × 75 g (3 oz) packet potato crisps, crushed
parsley sprigs to garnish

Put the flour into a bowl and gradually add the eggs, sugar, butter and milk, beating constantly to give a smooth mixture. Season with salt and pepper to taste and stir in the sweetcorn.

Spoon the mixture into an ovenproof dish and sprinkle the crisps over the top.

Bake in a preheated moderately hot oven, 190°C (375°F), Gas Mark 5, for 35 minutes until golden and firm. Serve hot, garnished with parsley.

Serves 4

POTATO AND CHEESE PIE

750 g (1½ lb) potatoes, boiled and mashed
salt and pepper
grated nutmeg
50 g (2 oz) butter
75 g (3 oz) Cheddar cheese, grated
TO GARNISH:
tomato slices
parsley sprigs

Season the potatoes with salt, pepper and nutmeg to taste and beat in half the butter. Spread the mixture in a shallow ovenproof dish. Top with the cheese and remaining butter.

Cook in a preheated moderate oven, 180°C (350°F), Gas Mark 4, for 15 minutes, then place under a preheated hot grill for 3 minutes.

Sprinkle with pepper and garnish with tomato and parsley. Serve hot.

Serves 4

LEFT: *Corn Fritters*
ABOVE: *Potato and Cheese Pie*

BEETROOT AND ORANGE SALAD

2 large oranges
4 tablespoons French Dressing (see page 15)
1 clove garlic, finely sliced (optional)
500 g (1 lb) cooked beetroot, sliced
watercress or mint sprigs to garnish

Grate the rind from one of the oranges and mix with the dressing. Add the garlic, if using. Peel and thinly slice both oranges, removing all pith.

Arrange the orange and beetroot slices in alternate layers in a serving dish. Pour the dressing over the top and garnish with watercress or mint sprigs. Chill before using.

Serves 4

Beetroot and Orange Salad

CARROT AND RAISIN SALAD

500 g (1 lb) carrots, grated
75 g (3 oz) raisins
2 tablespoons soy sauce
chopped parsley to garnish

Put the carrots and raisins into a serving dish and mix well.

Sprinkle over the soy sauce and toss well. Garnish with chopped parsley.

Serves 4

NOTE: As a variation, replace half the carrots with coarsely grated white cabbage.

CAULIFLOWER AND CRESS SALAD

500 g (1 lb) cauliflower
salt
1 carton mustard and cress, trimmed
25 g (1 oz) pumpkin seeds
4 tablespoons French Dressing (see page 15)

Break the cauliflower into florets and cook them in boiling salted water for 1 minute; drain and leave to cool completely. Place in a bowl with the remaining ingredients and toss thoroughly. Transfer to a shallow dish to serve.

Serves 4

TOMATOES WITH HORSERADISH MAYONNAISE

4 large tomatoes
3 tablespoons Mayonnaise (see page 21)
1 tablespoon creamed horseradish
1–2 tablespoons single cream (optional)
chopped parsley to garnish

Slice the tomatoes and arrange them in a serving dish. Mix the Mayonnaise with the horseradish, adding a little single cream if necessary to give the consistency of thick cream.

Spoon the dressing over the tomatoes and sprinkle with parsley.

Serves 4

KIDNEY BEAN SALAD

1 × 439 g ($15\frac{1}{2}$ oz) can red kidney beans, drained
1 × 425 g (15 oz) can cannellini beans, drained
1 × 397 g (14 oz) can artichoke hearts, drained and quartered
4 spring onions, chopped
2 celery sticks, chopped
1 small green pepper, cored, seeded and chopped
2 hard-boiled eggs, quartered
125 g (4 oz) streaky bacon, derinded to garnish

DRESSING:

1 clove garlic, crushed
120 ml (4 fl oz) Mayonnaise (see page 21)
1 tablespoon chopped parsley
1 tablespoon chopped basil
1 tablespoon chopped thyme
squeeze of lemon juice
salt and pepper
1 tablespoon capers (optional)

(Picture page 26)

Rinse the beans under cold water; leave to drain thoroughly.

Put the beans and artichokes into a salad bowl. Add the spring onions, celery and green pepper and arrange the eggs around the edge.

To make the dressing, mix the garlic, Mayonnaise, herbs and lemon juice together. Season well with salt and pepper and stir in the capers, if using. Spoon over the salad and toss well.

Cook the bacon under a preheated hot grill until crisp. Crumble and sprinkle over the salad. Serve immediately.

Serves 4

DATE AND NUT SALAD

175 g (6 oz) dates, stoned and halved
3 crisp dessert apples, cored and sliced
50 g (2 oz) walnut pieces
3 tablespoons lemon juice
1 × 150 g (5 oz) carton natural low-fat yogurt
salt

Put the dates, apples and walnuts into a serving bowl.

Mix together the lemon juice and yogurt. Add salt to taste. Pour over the salad and toss well until the ingredients are evenly coated.

Serves 4

Date and Nut Salad

SPANISH OMELETTE

3 tablespoons olive oil
2 onions, chopped
2 cloves garlic, crushed
1 red pepper, cored, seeded and chopped
4 eggs
salt and pepper
2 large potatoes, boiled and chopped
2 tablespoons chopped parsley

Heat 2 tablespoons of the oil in a 25 cm (10 inch) frying pan, add the onions and cook until softened. Add the garlic and red pepper; cook for 8 to 10 minutes, stirring occasionally.

Whisk the eggs, with salt and pepper to taste, in a bowl, then stir in the potatoes, parsley and fried vegetables.

Heat the remaining oil in the pan, pour in the egg mixture and spread evenly to the edge. Cook for about 5 minutes, shaking the pan to prevent the omelette sticking, until it comes away from the side of the pan.

Place the pan under a preheated moderate grill for about 3 minutes to cook the top. Slide the omelette onto a warmed serving plate and cut into wedges to serve.

Serves 4

SPINACH AND POTATO PATTIES

1 tablespoon oil
1 onion, chopped
1 clove garlic, crushed
250 g (8 oz) frozen chopped spinach, thawed and drained
500 g (1 lb) potatoes, boiled and mashed
¼ teaspoon ground nutmeg
125 g (4 oz) Cheddar cheese, grated
salt and pepper
wholewheat flour for coating
oil for shallow-frying

Heat the oil in a pan, add the onion and garlic and fry until softened. Squeeze the spinach dry and add to the pan with the potatoes, nutmeg, cheese, and salt and pepper to taste; mix thoroughly. Shape the mixture into 8 balls, using dampened hands, and flatten slightly.

Place some flour in a polythene bag, add the patties one at a time and shake to coat completely.

Fry in hot shallow oil for 2 minutes on each side, until golden brown.

Serve with salad and crusty bread.

Serves 3 to 4

HERRING AND APPLE SALAD

2 rollmops
few frisé leaves
2 red-skinned apples, cored
1 small onion, thinly sliced
150 ml (¼ pint) Soured Cream Dressing (see page 40)
ground paprika

Open out the rollmops, cut in half lengthways, then into 1 cm (½ inch) pieces.

Arrange the frisé leaves on individual serving dishes. Slice the apple thinly into rings.

Arrange the rollmops, apples and onion in layers over the frisé. Coat with the dressing and sprinkle with paprika to taste.

Serves 4

LEFT: *Spinach and Potato Patties*
RIGHT: *Egg, Croûton and Cress Salad; Piquant Winter Salad*

EGG, CROÛTON AND CRESS SALAD

oil for shallow-frying
6 slices white bread, cubed
4 hard-boiled eggs
2 bunches watercress
2 cartons mustard and cress
4 spring onions, chopped
1 green pepper, cored, seeded and chopped
salt and pepper

DRESSING:
50 g (2 oz) blue Brie cheese, softened
2 tablespoons Mayonnaise (see page 21)
2 tablespoons double cream
1 tablespoon chopped parsley
1 tablespoon chopped chives
pinch of chilli powder

Heat the oil in a frying pan, add the bread and fry until golden brown. Drain on kitchen paper.

Chop the eggs and put them into a large salad bowl. Break the watercress into sprigs and add it to the bowl with the mustard and cress, onions and green pepper. Season well with salt and pepper.

To make the dressing, put the cheese into a bowl and beat until smooth. Gradually mix in the Mayonnaise and cream, then fold in the herbs and chilli powder. Season with salt to taste.

Spoon the dressing over the salad. Add the croûtons, toss well and serve immediately.

Serves 4

PIQUANT WINTER SALAD

500 g (1 lb) small waxy potatoes
1 small onion, chopped
2 celery sticks, chopped
2 carrots, grated
2 heads chicory
125 g (4 oz) ham, sliced
50 g (2 oz) salami, diced
salt and pepper

DRESSING:
1 × 142 ml (5 fl oz) carton soured cream
2 tablespoons Mayonnaise (see page 21)
2 tablespoons chopped chives
1 teaspoon English made mustard
2 tablespoons green peppercorns
1 tablespoon chopped parsley
3 hard-boiled eggs, halved

Boil the potatoes, then carefully skin and slice them and place in a salad bowl. Add the onion, celery and carrots. Reserve a few chicory leaves for garnish. Slice the remaining chicory and add to the bowl with the ham and salami. Season with salt and pepper to taste and toss well.

To make the dressing, mix the soured cream, Mayonnaise, chives, mustard, peppercorns and parsley. Season with salt and pepper to taste.

Separate the egg whites from the yolks. Chop the whites and add to the dressing. Spoon over the salad and toss lightly.

Press the egg yolks through a sieve and sprinkle over the salad. Garnish with the chicory leaves to serve.

Serves 4

TOMATO AND ANCHOVY SALAD

4 hard-boiled eggs
1 tablespoon capers
2 tablespoons chopped gherkins
6 tomatoes, skinned and halved

DRESSING:
4 tablespoons French Dressing (see page 15)
2 tablespoons tomato ketchup
2 tablespoons chopped mixed herbs

TO GARNISH:
1 × 50 g (1¾ oz) can anchovies, drained and split lengthways
watercress sprigs

Slice the hard-boiled eggs and arrange in 4 individual shallow dishes. Sprinkle with the capers and gherkins. Place 3 tomato halves, cut side down, on each dish.

Put the dressing ingredients into a small bowl and mix together thoroughly. Spoon over the tomatoes to cover completely.

Arrange the anchovies in a cross on top of each tomato. Garnish with watercress to serve.

Serves 4

CRUDITÉS WITH AÏOLI

½ small cauliflower, broken into florets
4 carrots, cut into matchstick pieces
4 celery sticks, cut into matchstick pieces
1 green and 1 red pepper, cored, seeded and cut into matchstick pieces
250 g (8 oz) baby new potatoes, boiled

AÏOLI:
2 egg yolks
6 cloves garlic, crushed
½ teaspoon salt
300 ml (½ pint) olive oil
1–2 teaspoons lemon juice

To make the aïoli, beat the egg yolks with the garlic and salt to thicken. Add the oil drop by drop, beating constantly. As it thickens, add 1 teaspoon lemon juice, then add the oil in a steady stream, beating vigorously. Add the remaining lemon juice to taste and mix thoroughly.

Turn the aïoli into a small bowl, place on a large plate and surround with the vegetables.

Serves 4

NOTE: Aïoli is a Provençal dish. It should be very thick and smooth, with a powerful garlic flavour. Any combination of salad vegetables can be served as crudités; other possibilities are radishes, cucumber, courgettes and fennel.

CABBAGE SALAD WITH PEANUT DRESSING

1 small white cabbage
125 g (4 oz) salted peanuts, chopped
2 red peppers, cored, seeded and chopped
1 teaspoon anchovy essence
1 tablespoon soy sauce
2 tablespoons lemon juice
1 teaspoon chilli powder
½ teaspoon salt
1 teaspoon soft brown sugar
chopped parsley to garnish

Slice the cabbage finely and put into a salad bowl. Combine the remaining ingredients to form a crunchy sauce. Spoon over the cabbage, garnish with chopped parsley and serve immediately.

Serves 4

ASPARAGUS VINAIGRETTE

500 g (1 lb) asparagus
salt
4 tablespoons Lemon Vinaigrette Dressing (see page 37)
1 hard-boiled egg, halved
1 tablespoon chopped parsley to garnish

Cut the asparagus stalks all the same length, tie in bundles and place upright in a deep pan of boiling salted water. Make a lid with foil and dome it over the tips so that the heads cook in the steam. Small asparagus will take 15 minutes to cook; large stems up to 30 minutes. Drain very carefully, then arrange on a serving dish and leave to cool.

Spoon the dressing over the asparagus. Separate the egg white and yolk. Chop the egg white finely and sprinkle over the asparagus. Sieve the egg yolk over the top and sprinkle with the parsley.

Serves 4

PALM HEART AND AVOCADO VINAIGRETTE

few frisé leaves, torn into pieces
1 avocado
1 × 425 g (15 oz) can palm hearts, drained and quartered lengthways
3 tablespoons French Dressing (see page 15)
2 tablespoons sesame seeds, toasted

Arrange the frisé on 6 individual serving dishes. Halve, peel, stone and slice the avocado lengthways. Arrange the avocado and the palm hearts on the frisé. Pour over the dressing and sprinkle with the sesame seeds.

Serves 6

LEFT: *Crudités with Aïoli*
RIGHT: *Asparagus Vinaigrette; Palm Heart and Avocado Vinaigrette*

LEEKS VINAIGRETTE

8 thin leeks
salt
1 hard-boiled egg, finely chopped
1 tablespoon chopped parsley
4 tablespoons French Dressing (see page 15)
125 g (4 oz) streaky bacon, derinded and chopped

Trim the leeks, if necessary, to about 15 cm (6 inches); split lengthways as far as necessary to clean thoroughly.

Cook in boiling salted water for 8 minutes, until just tender. Drain well, arrange on individual serving dishes and leave to cool.

Add the egg and parsley to the dressing and spoon over the leeks. Fry the bacon in its own fat until crisp, then sprinkle over the leeks.

Serves 4

LAMB'S LETTUCE SALAD

250 (8 oz) lamb's lettuce
1 head of radicchio, torn into pieces
1 head of chicory, sliced diagonally into 1 cm (½ inch) pieces
½ fennel bulb, thickly sliced
few dandelion leaves, halved (optional)
2 tablespoons chopped parsley
50 g (2 oz) shelled walnuts
6 tablespoons French Dressing (see page 15)

Put the lamb's lettuce leaves into a salad bowl. Add the radicchio, chicory and fennel with the remaining ingredients and toss thoroughly.

Serves 6 to 8

NOTE: Lamb's lettuce or corn salad is a mild-flavoured salad plant which is easy to grow in the garden. The leaves are fragile and must be treated gently. Frisé may be used in place of lamb's lettuce.

BEANSPROUT AND CRESS SALAD

125 g (4 oz) Chinese leaves, thinly sliced
125 g (4 oz) beansprouts, separated
2 cartons salad cress
6 spring onions, sliced
6 tablespoons Vinaigrette Dressing (see page 37)

Put the Chinese leaves into a salad bowl. Add the beansprouts with the cress and spring onions; mix well.

Pour over the dressing and toss well just before serving.

Serves 4 to 6

BABY TOMATOES WITH AVOCADO DRESSING

500 g (1 lb) baby tomatoes, skinned
150 ml (¼ pint) Avocado Dressing (see page 37)
1 tablespoon chopped parsley

Pile the tomatoes onto a shallow serving dish. Pour over the dressing and sprinkle with the parsley.

Serves 4

Lamb's Lettuce Salad; Beansprout and Cress Salad

FRISÉ AND GRUYÈRE SALAD

1 head of frisé, torn into pieces
75 g (3 oz) Gruyère cheese, diced
25 g (1 oz) hazelnuts, chopped and browned
75 g (3 oz) smoked ham, diced
4 tablespoons French Dressing (see page 15)
1 tablespoon chopped parsley

Put the frisé into a bowl with the cheese, nuts and ham. Pour over the dressing and toss thoroughly. Transfer to a salad bowl and sprinkle with the parsley.
Serves 6 to 8

VINAIGRETTE DRESSING

175 ml (6 fl oz) olive oil
4 tablespoons cider vinegar
1 teaspoon clear honey
1 clove garlic, crushed
2 tablespoons chopped mixed herbs (e.g. mint, parsley, chives, thyme)
salt and pepper

Put all the ingredients into a screw-topped jar, adding salt and pepper to taste. Shake well to blend before using.
Makes 250 ml (8 fl oz)
LEMON VINAIGRETTE: use 4 tablespoons fresh lemon juice in place of the cider vinegar.

AVOCADO DRESSING

1 medium avocado
5 tablespoons single cream
1 teaspoon Worcestershire sauce
150 ml (¼ pint) Soured Cream Dressing (see page 40)

Halve, peel, stone and slice the avocado and put it into an electric blender or food processor with the cream and Worcestershire sauce. Blend until smooth, then combine with the Soured Cream Dressing.
Makes 350 ml (12 fl oz)

PEPPER AND SALAMI SALAD

2 each large green, red and yellow peppers
6 tomatoes, thickly sliced
4 hard-boiled eggs, thickly sliced
50 g (2 oz) salami, chopped
50 g (2 oz) salami, chopped
2 × 50 g (1¾ oz) cans anchovy fillets, drained
24 black olives
DRESSING:
2 cloves garlic, crushed
1 tablespoon chopped parsley
1 tablespoon chopped chives
1 tablespoon chopped chervil
1 tablespoon chopped tarragon
1 teaspoon coarse grain mustard
1 teaspoon clear honey
3 tablespoons lemon juice
6 tablespoons olive oil
salt and pepper

Place the whole peppers under a preheated hot grill until the skins are charred. Leave to cool, then peel away the skin, remove the cores and seeds, and slice the flesh.

Arrange the tomatoes and eggs in a salad bowl. Sprinkle in the garlic sausage and salami. Place the peppers around the edge.

Arrange the anchovy fillets in a lattice over the salad and place the olives on top.

Mix the dressing ingredients together in a bowl, seasoning with salt and pepper to taste. Spoon over the salad.

Chill for 20 minutes before serving.
Serves 4

Pepper and Salami Salad

Caesar Salad

CAESAR SALAD

2 cloves garlic, crushed
6 tablespoons olive oil
3 slices bread, cut into 5 mm (¼ inch) cubes
2 tablespoons lemon juice
1 teaspoon Worcestershire sauce
salt and pepper
1 large cos lettuce, torn into pieces
2 eggs, boiled for 1 minute
4 tablespoons grated Parmesan cheese

Place the garlic in the olive oil and leave to soak for 3 to 4 hours. Strain the oil.

Fry the bread in 4 tablespoons of the garlic-flavoured oil until golden. Drain on kitchen paper.

Pour the remaining oil into a small bowl with the lemon juice, Worcestershire sauce, and salt and pepper to taste and mix well.

Put the lettuce into a salad bowl. Pour over the prepared dressing and toss well.

Break the eggs over the lettuce, scraping out the partly set egg white, and mix thoroughly to combine the egg with the dressing.

Add the cheese and croûtons and give a final toss just before serving.

Serves 6

NOTE: This salad was created by an Italian, Caesar Cardini, for his restaurant in Tijuana, Mexico. It has subsequently acquired an international reputation.

ONION AND WATERMELON VINAIGRETTE

1 kg (2 lb) watermelon, seeded and cut into wedges
1 tablespoon chopped mint
1 Spanish onion, thinly sliced
3 tablespoons Lemon Vinaigrette Dressing (see page 37)

Slice the watermelon wedges diagonally into strips. Put into a bowl and sprinkle with the mint.

Mix the onion and dressing together in another bowl and leave for 1 hour, stirring occasionally.

Mix the onion and dressing with the watermelon and transfer to a serving bowl.

Serves 4 to 6

NOTE: This unusual and refreshing salad is delicious served as an accompaniment to rich meats.

TOMATO AND BASIL SALAD

500 g (1 lb) beefsteak tomatoes, thinly sliced
salt and pepper
3 tablespoons olive oil
2 tablespoons chopped basil

Lay the tomato slices in a shallow serving dish, sprinkling each layer with salt and pepper. Pour over the oil and sprinkle with the basil.

Serves 4

NOTE: The piquant flavour of basil greatly enhances the flavour of the tomatoes, and the mellowness of the olive oil brings out the full flavour of this delicious salad. Serve as a tasty main course accompaniment or a refreshing summer first course.

RIGHT: *Chicken Liver and Spinach Salad; Curried Chicken Salad*

CHICKEN LIVER AND SPINACH SALAD

250 g (8 oz) spinach, stalks trimmed
3 tablespoons French Dressing (see page 15)
2 tablespoons olive oil
1 × 125 g (4 oz) bacon steak, cut into 5 mm (¼ inch) wide strips
4 chicken livers, cut into strips
2 tablespoons cider vinegar
pepper

Wash and dry the spinach leaves thoroughly, then cut into strips. Put into a salad bowl, pour over the dressing, toss well and leave for 10 minutes.

Heat 1 tablespoon of the oil in a pan, add the bacon and fry until golden. Put on top of the spinach.

Heat the remaining oil in the pan, add the chicken livers and fry for 3 to 4 minutes, until well browned. Add to the salad bowl.

Add the vinegar to the pan and stir to blend with any remaining juices. Pour over the salad, season well with pepper, and toss thoroughly.

Serve with crusty bread for a light lunch.

Serves 4

CURRIED CHICKEN SALAD

3 celery sticks, cut into small strips
350 g (12 oz) cooked chicken, skinned and cut into strips
1 × 227 g (8 oz) can pineapple pieces, drained
50 g (2 oz) split almonds, browned
6 tablespoons Mayonnaise (see page 21)
4 tablespoons natural low-fat yogurt
1 teaspoon curry paste
1 tablespoon tomato ketchup
few lettuce leaves

Put the celery into a bowl with the chicken, pineapple and almonds. Toss the ingredients together.

Mix the Mayonnaise, yogurt, curry paste and tomato ketchup together, pour over the chicken salad and mix thoroughly.

Place the lettuce on a serving dish and spoon the chicken mixture into the centre.

Serves 4 to 6

Salmon and Dill Salad

SWEDISH HERRING SALAD

- *4 rollmops*
- *125 g (4 oz) cooked beetroot, diced*
- *250 g (8 oz) cooked potato, diced*
- *1 small onion, chopped*
- *2 dill cucumbers, chopped*
- *150 ml ($\frac{1}{4}$ pint) Soured Cream Dressing (see right)*
- *2 hard-boiled eggs, chopped*
- *1 tablespoon chopped dill or fennel to garnish*

Unroll the rollmops, cut in half lengthways, then cut into thin strips. Put into a bowl with the beetroot, potato, onion and dill cucumber and mix well. Pour over the dressing and toss thoroughly.

Transfer the salad to a shallow serving dish. Sprinkle the eggs over the salad. Garnish with the dill or fennel.

Serves 4

SALMON AND DILL SALAD

- *2 tablespoons fine sea salt*
- *2 tablespoons caster sugar*
- *1 teaspoon ground black pepper*
- *2 tablespoons chopped dill*
- *750 g ($1\frac{1}{2}$ lb) tail piece of salmon, filleted*
- *1 fennel bulb*
- *2 tablespoons Lemon Vinaigrette Dressing (see page 37)*

DILL DRESSING:

- *2 tablespoons German mustard*
- *1 tablespoon caster sugar*
- *1 tablespoon wine vinegar*
- *6 tablespoons olive oil*
- *2 tablespoons soured cream*
- *2 tablespoons chopped dill*

Mix together the salt, sugar, pepper and dill and sprinkle half the mixture over the base of a shallow dish. Lay the salmon on top and sprinkle with the remaining dill mixture. Cover and leave to marinate for 2 to 3 days in the refrigerator, turning the salmon each day.

Trim the stalks, base and coarse outer leaves from the fennel; reserve a few feathery leaves for garnish. Cut the bulb in half lengthways, then slice very thinly into strips. Put into a bowl and pour over the vinaigrette. Toss well and leave to marinate for 1 hour.

To make the Dill Dressing, beat the mustard, sugar and vinegar together. Gradually add the oil, beating well between each addition. Gradually beat in the cream, then stir in the dill.

Remove the skin from the salmon. Cut the fish into 3 mm ($\frac{1}{8}$ inch) wide strips, across the grain. Arrange on a serving dish. Pour over the Dill Dressing and arrange the fennel strips around the edge. Garnish with the fennel leaves. Serve with rye bread.

Serves 4

NOTE: This is a version of the well-known Scandinavian dish, Gravad Lax. Serve it on a special occasion.

SOURED CREAM DRESSING

- *1 × 142 ml (5 fl oz) carton soured cream*
- *1 tablespoon lemon juice*
- *1 clove garlic, crushed*
- *1 teaspoon clear honey*
- *salt and pepper*
- *milk (optional)*

Put all the ingredients into a bowl, adding salt and pepper to taste, and mix thoroughly with a fork. Add milk to thin if necessary.

Makes 150 ml ($\frac{1}{4}$ pint)

CHICKEN AND AVOCADO SALAD

2 avocados
2–3 teaspoons lemon juice
250 g (8 oz) cooked chicken, cut into pieces
1 × 230 g (7½ oz) can water chestnuts, drained and sliced
6 tablespoons natural low-fat yogurt
½ teaspoon Worcestershire sauce
salt and pepper
6 tablespoons Mayonnaise (see page 21)

Halve, stone and peel the avocados. Slice one of them. Reserve 3 slices and brush with some of the lemon juice.

Put the remaining sliced avocado into a bowl, pour over the remaining lemon juice and toss well to prevent the avocado discolouring. Add the chicken and water chestnuts and mix together.

Put the remaining avocado halves into an electric blender or food processor with the yogurt, Worcestershire sauce, and salt and pepper to taste. Blend until smooth, then add to the Mayonnaise and mix thoroughly.

Pour the dressing over the chicken mixture and toss well to combine. Spoon onto a shallow serving dish and garnish with the reserved avocado slices.

Serves 4

Chicken and Avocado Salad

WALDORF SALAD

juice of 1 lemon
500 g (1 lb) red dessert apples, cored and sliced
1 head of celery, sliced
150 ml (¼ pint) Mayonnaise (see page 21)
1 teaspoon caster sugar
75 g (3 oz) walnuts, roughly chopped
1 crisp lettuce

Put the lemon juice into a large mixing bowl, add the apples and toss quickly to prevent them discolouring. Set aside a few apple slices for garnish.

Add the celery, Mayonnaise, sugar and walnuts to the bowl and mix well; make sure all the ingredients are thoroughly combined.

Arrange the lettuce in a salad bowl and pile the salad on top. Garnish with the reserved apple slices and serve immediately.

Serves 4 to 6

CRAB AND AVOCADO SALAD

350 g (12 oz) crab claw meat, chopped or 2 × 177 g (6 oz) cans crabmeat, drained and chopped
150 ml (¼ pint) Avocado Dressing (see page 37)
2 avocados
2 tablespoons French Dressing (see page 15)
1 tablespoon pumpkin seeds (optional)

Put the crabmeat into a bowl, pour over half the avocado dressing and mix well.

Halve, stone and peel the avocados. Slice them lengthways and arrange cut side down on a serving dish, pressing lightly to separate the slices out to the edge of the dish. Brush with the French dressing.

Spoon the crab into the centre, coat with the remaining avocado dressing and sprinkle with the pumpkin seeds, if using.

Serves 4

French-Style Green Beans

STUFFED MUSHROOMS

8 large flat mushrooms
50 g (2 oz) butter
1 slice white bread, crusts removed
1 tablespoon chopped parsley
1 clove garlic, crushed
4 shallots or small onions, chopped
salt and pepper
4 tablespoons dry white wine
parsley sprigs to garnish

Remove the mushroom stalks and chop them finely. Melt half the butter in a pan, add the mushroom caps and cook for 5 minutes. Remove from the pan and set aside.

Soak the bread in water for a few minutes, then squeeze almost dry and put into a bowl.

Melt the remaining butter in the pan, add the chopped mushroom stalks, parsley, garlic and shallots or onions and cook for 5 minutes. Season with salt and pepper to taste and pour in the wine. Increase the heat and cook for 2 minutes. Stir into the bread.

Arrange the mushroom caps in an ovenproof dish and fill with the mixture. Cover and cook in a preheated moderate oven, 180°C (350°F), Gas Mark 4, for 20 minutes. Serve hot, garnished with parsley.

Serves 4

FRENCH-STYLE GREEN BEANS

100 g (3½ oz) butter
2 bunches spring onions, cut into 5 cm (2 inch) lengths
1 kg (2 lb) small French beans
salt and pepper
1 crisp lettuce, quartered
1 bunch of mixed herbs (including parsley and chervil), tied together

Melt the butter in a pan, add the spring onions and cook for 2 minutes. Add the beans and cook for 20 minutes. Season with salt and pepper to taste. Add the lettuce and herbs and cook for 5 minutes.

Remove the herbs and transfer the bean mixture to a warmed serving dish. Serve immediately.

Serves 4

WHITE BEANS WITH TOMATOES

2 × 425 g (15 oz) cans cannellini beans, drained
3 tablespoons olive oil
2 cloves garlic, crushed
½ teaspoon dried sage
1 × 227 g (8 oz) can peeled tomatoes, drained
salt and pepper

Rinse the beans with cold water and drain.

Heat the oil, garlic and sage together gently in a saucepan for 1 to 2 minutes, then stir in the beans.

Press the tomatoes through a sieve into the pan. Add salt and pepper to taste and stir gently. Cover and simmer for 10 minutes.

Serve hot as a vegetable, or cold topped with tuna as an antipasto.

Serves 4

NOTE: If cannellini beans are unobtainable use 175 g (6 oz) dried haricot beans soaked overnight, boiled rapidly for 10 minutes, and then cooked for 1½ to 2 hours until tender. Drain and use in the same way as cannellini beans.

TUSCAN BAKED FENNEL

625 g (1¼ lb) fennel bulbs, cut vertically into 2 cm (¾ inch) thick pieces
salt and pepper
1 thick slice lemon
1 tablespoon oil
25 g (1 oz) butter
25 g (1 oz) grated Parmesan cheese
fennel leaves to garnish (optional)

Put the sliced fennel into a pan with a pinch of salt, the lemon and oil and add sufficient boiling water to cover. Cook for 20 minutes or until just tender. Drain well.

Melt the butter in a gratin dish or shallow flameproof casserole, add the fennel and turn to coat. Season to taste with pepper and sprinkle with cheese.

Place under a preheated grill until lightly browned. Serve immediately, garnished with fennel leaves, if liked.

Serves 4

SEAFOOD SALAD

16 fresh mussels, scrubbed clean
4 shelled scallops, quartered
350 g (12 oz) haddock fillets
150 ml (¼ pint) dry white wine
150 ml (¼ pint) fish stock
1 bay leaf
1 bouquet garni
salt and pepper
1 × 177 g (6 oz) can crabmeat, drained
2 small lettuces

DRESSING:
120 ml (4 fl oz) Mayonnaise (see page 21)
1 tablespoon chopped chives
1 tablespoon chopped parsley
1 clove garlic, crushed (optional)
2 eggs, hard-boiled, chopped
2 celery sticks, chopped
¼ cucumber, diced

Discard any mussels that are open. Put the closed mussels into a shallow pan with the scallops and haddock and pour over the wine and stock. Add the herbs and season well with salt and pepper. Bring to the boil and cook for 4 minutes, until the mussels have opened and the haddock is tender. Carefully remove from the stock, discarding any mussels that have not opened. Remove the shells. Place all the fish, except the crabmeat, in a bowl, cover and leave to cool.

Put the Mayonnaise, herbs and garlic, if using, into a mixing bowl, and season well with salt and pepper. Add the eggs and celery to the bowl.

Add the crabmeat to the cooled fish, then spoon over the dressing and mix well. Separate the lettuces into leaves, arrange in individual serving dishes and pile the fish mixture in the centre to serve.

Serves 4

NOTE: Canned mussels can be used in place of fresh ones; add them to the salad with the crabmeat.

HARICOT BEAN AND TUNA SALAD

½ lettuce
4 large tomatoes, chopped
50 g (2 oz) black olives, halved and stoned
1 clove garlic, crushed
8 tablespoons cooked haricot beans
3 hard-boiled eggs, quartered
1 × 198 g (7 oz) can tuna steak, drained
chopped chives to garnish

DRESSING:
3 tablespoons olive oil
1½ tablespoons white wine vinegar
salt and pepper
½ teaspoon French mustard

Arrange the lettuce in a large salad bowl and pile the remaining salad ingredients on top.

Put the dressing ingredients into a screw-topped jar and shake well. Pour over the salad and toss well.

Sprinkle with chives and serve immediately.

Serves 4

Haricot Bean and Tuna Salad

ITALIAN MIXED SALAD

1 crisp lettuce, torn into pieces or 125 g (4 oz) young spinach leaves
½ green pepper, cored, seeded and sliced
2 under-ripe tomatoes, sliced
½ small cucumber, sliced
6 radishes, sliced
DRESSING:
3 tablespoons olive oil
2 teaspoons lemon juice
1 clove garlic, crushed
salt and pepper

Put the lettuce or spinach leaves into a salad bowl and top with the remaining vegetables.

Put the dressing ingredients into a screw-topped jar, adding salt and pepper to taste, and shake well.

Sprinkle the dressing over the salad and toss lightly together. Serve immediately.

Serves 4

NOTE: Raw young spinach leaves are widely used for salads in Italy – when available, they make a nice change from lettuce. For a really crisp salad, after washing and thoroughly drying the lettuce or spinach, place it in a polythene bag and leave in the refrigerator for a few hours.

FENNEL SALAD

1 large fennel bulb, cut vertically into thin slices
½ large cucumber, diced
4 radishes, sliced
2 oranges, peeled and divided into segments
DRESSING:
2 tablespoons olive oil
2 teaspoons lemon juice
1 clove garlic, crushed
2 teaspoons chopped mint
salt and pepper

Cut the fennel slices into strips and put into a salad bowl with the cucumber, radishes and orange segments.

Put the dressing ingredients into a screw-topped jar, adding salt and pepper to taste, and shake well. Sprinkle over the vegetables and toss lightly. Serve immediately.

Serves 4

Italian Mixed Salad; Fennel Salad

ITALIAN CAULIFLOWER SALAD

1 cauliflower, broken into florets
salt and pepper
5 tablespoons olive oil
1½ tablespoons wine vinegar
1 tablespoon capers, drained
1 tablespoon chopped parsley
few black olives
1 × 50 g (1¾ oz) can anchovy fillets, drained and sliced

Put the cauliflower into boiling salted water and cook until tender but still firm, about 5 to 6 minutes. Drain and rinse under running cold water.

Mix the oil, vinegar and a little salt and pepper together in a salad bowl. Add the cauliflower and toss gently. Sprinkle with the capers, parsley and olives. Arrange the anchovy fillets in a lattice pattern on top. Serve immediately.

Serves 4

POTATO AND SORREL SALAD

500 g (1 lb) boiled waxy potatoes
2 tablespoons French Dressing (see page 15)
2 hard-boiled eggs, cut into eighths
4 tomatoes, skinned, seeded and cut into eighths
few sorrel leaves, finely shredded
3 tablespoons Mayonnaise (see page 21)
3 tablespoons natural low-fat yogurt

Chop the potatoes roughly into a mixing bowl while still warm and pour over the dressing. Toss thoroughly and leave to cool.

Add the eggs, tomatoes and sorrel to the potatoes and toss well. Transfer to a serving dish.

Mix together the Mayonnaise and yogurt and spoon over the salad.

Serves 4

NOTE: A small quantity of sorrel makes an excellent addition to a rich salad and gives a pleasant piquant flavour. If you have no sorrel, use spinach or dandelion leaves instead.

Italian Cauliflower Salad

RICE SALAD

250 g (8 oz) easy-cook Italian rice
2 teaspoons salt
600 ml (1 pint) cold water
4 tablespoons olive oil
1 tablespoon wine vinegar
2 spring onions, finely chopped
1 small green pepper, cored, seeded and thinly sliced
salt and pepper
¼ cucumber, diced
2 tablespoons chopped parsley
crisp lettuce leaves

Put the rice, salt and water into a pan and bring to the boil. Stir, cover tightly and simmer gently for 15 minutes. Uncover and cook for 1 to 2 minutes until the liquid is completely absorbed.

Combine the oil, vinegar, spring onions, green pepper, and plenty of salt and pepper in a bowl. Add the hot rice and toss together thoroughly. Cover and leave until cold.

Just before serving, stir in the cucumber and parsley. Line a shallow bowl with lettuce, pile the rice salad in the centre and serve immediately.

Serves 4 to 6

FISH DISHES

Whether your taste is for simple plaice or exotic shellfish and whether you are looking for a new way with canned salmon or tuna or for something rather more special, you will find the answer in this chapter. We have fish dishes to suit all purses and occasions, from simple snacks to substantial main course dishes.

For mid-week eating, try pan-fried trout sprinkled with toasted almonds; a fluffy prawn pilaff with onions, rice, tomatoes and basil; or stir-fried cod with peas, sweetcorn and bacon made all the more tasty with sherry, soy sauce and stock.

When impressions count, then push out the boat with a simple yet sophisticated starter of scallops sautéed in butter with garlic and parsley; or a main course dish of spicy seafood cooked in a rich and exotic sauce of wine, cream, shallots and mustard, or treat your guests to a taste of India with an aromatic seafood curry nestling on a bed of rice.

And don't forget the great outdoors where fish is perhaps the simplest food to prepare and cook on a barbecue or grill. Sizzling marinated prawns and grilled mackerel, whiting, trout or red mullet, skewered or scored, then cooked to golden perfection, can be the ideal food for quick summertime eating.

Whatever the season or occasion remember, whenever you buy fish, that freshness is of paramount importance. Always choose fresh-smelling fish and shellfish with moist, compact flesh, clear, shiny eyes and a firm texture for assured quality.

SCALLOPS WITH GARLIC AND PARSLEY

75 g (3 oz) butter
3 cloves garlic
12 shelled fresh scallops or frozen scallops, thawed
2 tablespoons chopped parsley
salt and pepper

Melt the butter in a pan, add the garlic and fry until browned; discard.

Add the coral and white scallop flesh to the pan and cook for 5 minutes. Sprinkle in the parsley, and salt and pepper to taste. Pile into warmed individual serving dishes and serve immediately.

Serves 4

BELOW: *Scallops with Garlic and Parsley; Trout with Almonds*
RIGHT: *Moules à la Marinière; Sole Véronique*

TROUT WITH ALMONDS

4 trout, cleaned, with heads and tails intact
salt and pepper
75 g (3 oz) butter
50 g (2 oz) flaked almonds
juice of 1 lemon
TO GARNISH:
lemon slices
parsley sprigs

Season the fish with salt and pepper. Melt the butter in a frying pan, add the trout and fry for 6 minutes on each side until golden and cooked through. Arrange on a warmed serving dish and keep hot.

Fry the almonds in the butter remaining in the pan until golden. Add the lemon juice and spoon over the fish. Garnish with lemon and parsley and serve immediately.

Serves 4

VARIATION: Use cashew nuts instead of the flaked almonds.

MOULES À LA MARINIÈRE

50 g (2 oz) butter, softened
6 shallots or small onions, finely chopped
1 bouquet garni
450 ml ($\frac{3}{4}$ pint) dry white wine
salt and pepper
2.75 kg (6 lb) or 6 pints fresh mussels, scrubbed clean
25 g (1 oz) plain flour
chopped parsley to garnish

Melt half the butter in a pan, add the shallots or small onions and fry gently until golden. Add the bouquet garni, wine, and salt and pepper to taste. Bring to the boil. Discard any open mussels. Put the closed mussels into the boiling liquid.

Cover and simmer for about 5 minutes until the shells open; discard any that do not. Remove the mussels from the pan with a slotted spoon and pile into a warmed serving dish. Keep hot.

Bring the sauce to the boil and boil until reduced by half. Remove the bouquet garni.

Blend the remaining butter with the flour, divide into small pieces and add gradually to the stock, stirring all the time until dissolved. Bring to the boil, stirring, then simmer for 2 minutes. Pour over the mussels and sprinkle with parsley.

Serves 6

SOLE VÉRONIQUE

750 g ($1\frac{1}{2}$ lb) sole or plaice fillets, skinned
2 shallots or small onions, chopped
1 sprig parsley
1 bay leaf
150 ml ($\frac{1}{4}$ pint) dry white wine
1 tablespoon lemon juice
salt and pepper
15 g ($\frac{1}{2}$ oz) butter
2 tablespoons plain flour
5 tablespoons milk
1 tablespoon cream
175 g (6 oz) grapes, halved, deseeded and skinned

Fold the fillets in half and arrange in a buttered ovenproof dish. Sprinkle with the chopped shallots or onions, parsley, bay leaf, wine, lemon juice, and salt and pepper to taste. Add just enough water to cover the fish.

Cook in a preheated moderate oven, 180°C (350°F), Gas Mark 4, for 15 to 20 minutes until tender. Transfer the fillets to a warmed serving dish, using a slotted spoon. Keep warm. Strain the stock.

Melt the butter in a pan, stir in the flour and cook for 1 minute. Gradually stir in the stock and enough milk to make a smooth pouring sauce. Adjust the seasoning and stir in the cream and grapes. Spoon over the fish and serve immediately.

Serves 4

Fish in White Wine

TROUT WITH HAM AND GARLIC

4 slices Parma ham or other raw smoked ham, fat removed
4 trout, cleaned, with heads and tails intact
salt and pepper
4 tablespoons olive oil
2 cloves garlic, thinly sliced
grated rind and juice of 1 lemon
2 tablespoons chopped parsley
TO GARNISH:
lemon wedges
parsley sprigs

Roll up the ham and place one piece inside the cavity of each trout. Season each fish liberally with salt and pepper.

Heat the oil in a frying pan, add the garlic and 2 trout and fry for 5 to 8 minutes on each side, until cooked. Drain on kitchen paper and keep hot while cooking the other trout. Add the lemon rind and juice to the pan and cook for 1 minute.

Arrange the trout on warmed dishes and spoon over the garlic and lemon flavoured oil. Sprinkle with the chopped parsley and serve immediately, garnished with lemon wedges and parsley sprigs.

Serves 4

PRAWNS IN SHERRY

50 g (2 oz) butter
1 clove garlic, crushed
1 small onion, finely chopped
salt and pepper
150 ml (¼ pint) medium dry sherry
300 ml (½ pint) double cream
750 g (1½ lb) cooked shelled prawns
TO GARNISH:
chopped parsley
1 cooked unshelled prawn (optional)

Melt the butter in a frying pan, add the garlic and onion and fry until softened but not browned. Season with salt and pepper to taste. Pour in the sherry. Bring to the boil and boil until most of the liquid has evaporated. Add the cream and simmer until thickened. Check the seasoning and stir in the prawns.

Pile the mixture into a serving dish, sprinkle with parsley and garnish with a whole prawn if using. Serve immediately.

Serves 6

FISH IN WHITE WINE

50 g (2 oz) butter
2 tablespoons chopped spring onions
1.25 kg (2½ lb) sole or plaice fillets, skinned
salt and pepper
1 small bunch of parsley
450 ml (¾ pint) dry white wine
2 tablespoons plain flour
125 g (4 oz) cooked shelled prawns
TO GARNISH:
lemon wedges
few cooked unshelled prawns (optional)

Melt half the butter in a pan, add the spring onions and cook for 2 minutes.

Roll up the fish fillets and arrange in an ovenproof dish. Sprinkle with the spring onions, and salt and pepper to taste. Add the parlsey and wine. Cover and cook in a preheated moderate oven, 160°C (325°F), Gas Mark 3 for 15 to 20 minutes until tender. Transfer the fish to a warmed serving dish using a slotted spoon and keep warm; reserve the stock.

Combine the remaining butter and flour to make a paste. Strain the stock into a pan and bring to the boil. Stir in the paste, a little at a time, to thicken the sauce, beating after each addition. Add the prawns and check the seasoning. Spoon over the fish and garnish with lemon wedges and whole prawns, if using.

Serves 6

GRILLED SCAMPI

500 g (1 lb) frozen scampi, just thawed and dried
4 tablespoons olive oil
50 g (2 oz) dry white breadcrumbs
½ clove garlic, crushed
1 tablespoon finely chopped parsley
salt and pepper
lemon wedges to garnish

Put the scampi into a bowl with the oil, breadcrumbs, garlic, parsley and salt and pepper to taste. Stir gently until thoroughly coated. Cover and leave to marinate for 30 minutes at room temperature.

Thread onto 4 kebab skewers, pushing them to the centre. Cook under a preheated very hot grill for 2 to 3 minutes on each side, depending on size, until the crumbs are crisp. Serve immediately, with lemon wedges.

Serves 4

Grilled Scampi; Marinated Grilled Fish

MARINATED GRILLED FISH

4 small mackerel, whiting, trout, or mullet, cleaned
salt and pepper
2 rosemary sprigs or bay leaves
4 tablespoons olive oil
1 tablespoon lemon juice
1 small clove garlic, crushed (optional)
lemon wedges to garnish

Make 3 cuts across each side of the fish. Sprinkle with salt and pepper. Put the herbs into a shallow dish and lay the fish on top. Mix together the oil, lemon juice and garlic, if using, and pour over the fish. Cover and chill for 3 to 4 hours, turning several times.

Transfer the fish to the grill rack. Place about 10 cm (4 inches) away from a preheated moderate grill and cook for 5 to 6 minutes on each side, until cooked through and golden.

Serve immediately, garnished with lemon wedges.

Serves 4

PRAWN PILAFF

50 g (2 oz) butter
1 small onion, finely chopped
1 clove garlic, crushed
250 g (8 oz) long-grain rice
200 ml ($\frac{1}{3}$ pint) dry white wine
2–3 strands of saffron
600 ml (1 pint) fish or chicken stock (approximately)
salt and pepper
4 tomatoes, skinned, seeded and chopped
1 tablespoon chopped basil
250 g (8 oz) peeled prawns
TO GARNISH:
basil leaves
few whole prawns (optional)
grated Parmesan cheese

Melt the butter in a pan, add the onion and garlic and cook gently for 5 minutes. Add the rice and toss until coated in the butter. Add the wine and saffron. Cook until most of the wine has evaporated, stirring constantly.

Stir in two-thirds of the stock and season with salt and pepper to taste. Bring to the boil, cover and simmer for 10 to 12 minutes until the rice is just tender, stirring occasionally; add more stock if required, to keep the rice slightly moist and ensure it does not burn. Stir in the tomatoes, basil and prawns and cook for 2 minutes.

Pile the pilaff into a warmed serving dish. Garnish with basil and whole prawns, if using. Serve with Parmesan cheese.

Serves 6

GOLDEN BAKED FISH

4 cod, hake or haddock steaks
salt and pepper
50 g (2 oz) dry white breadcrumbs
50 g (2 oz) grated Parmesan cheese
MARINADE:
4 tablespoons olive oil
1 small clove garlic, crushed
2 mint or parsley sprigs, finely chopped
$\frac{1}{4}$ teaspoon dried oregano
TO GARNISH:
lemon quarters
parsley or mint sprigs

Combine the marinade ingredients in a shallow dish. Season the fish with salt and pepper and place in the marinade, turning to coat. Cover and leave in the refrigerator for 3 to 4 hours, turning once. Drain, reserving the marinade.

Mix together the breadcrumbs and cheese and use to coat the fish, pressing on firmly.

Strain the marinade into an ovenproof dish and add the fish. Spoon over enough marinade to moisten the coating. Cook in a preheated moderately hot oven, 190°C (375°F), Gas Mark 5, for 20 to 25 minutes. Garnish with lemon and herbs to serve.

Serves 4

FISH IN WHOLEWHEAT BREADCRUMBS

4 haddock fillets
2 tablespoons plain flour
125 g (4 oz) wholewheat dry breadcrumbs
2 tablespoons chopped parsley
salt and pepper
1 egg, beaten
oil for shallow-frying
TO GARNISH:
parsley sprigs
lemon wedges

Dip the fillets into the flour.

Mix together the breadcrumbs, parsley, and salt and pepper to taste on a plate.

Dip the fillets into the beaten egg, then into the breadcrumb mixture. Shallow-fry in hot oil until crisp and golden.

Garnish with parsley and lemon and serve with tartare sauce.

Serves 4

LEFT: *Prawn Pilaff*
RIGHT: *Trout with Mushrooms; Sole with Courgettes*

TROUT WITH MUSHROOMS

flour for coating
salt and pepper
4 trout, cleaned
2 tablespoons oil
65 g (2½ oz) butter
3 spring onions (green part only), chopped
350 g (12 oz) button mushrooms
1 tablespoon lemon juice
1 tablespoon chopped parsley
25 g (1 oz) dry white breadcrumbs
lemon wedges to garnish

Season the flour with salt and pepper and use to coat the trout.

Heat the oil and 25 g (1 oz) of the butter in a large frying pan, add the trout and fry gently for 6 minutes on each side until cooked and golden.

Meanwhile, melt the remaining butter in a pan, add the spring onion tops and mushrooms and fry for 3 minutes until the mushrooms begin to soften. Stir in the lemon juice, parsley and a little salt.

Arrange the trout and mushroom mixture on a warmed serving dish and keep hot.

Quickly fry the breadcrumbs in the fat remaining in the pan until crisp. Sprinkle over the fish and garnish with lemon wedges.

Serves 4

SOLE WITH COURGETTES

4 tablespoons oil
1 onion, finely chopped
250 g (8 oz) tomatoes, skinned and chopped
1 teaspoon tomato purée
½ teaspoon dried basil
salt and pepper
4 small courgettes, thinly sliced
flour for coating
4 × 175 g (6 oz) sole fillets
25 g (1 oz) butter
2 tablespoons grated Parmesan cheese

Heat half the oil in a pan, add the onion and fry gently until soft. Add the tomatoes, tomato purée, basil and a little salt and pepper. Simmer, covered, for 5 minutes. Add the courgettes and simmer for 8 minutes, or until just tender.

Season the flour with salt and pepper and use to coat the fish. Heat the remaining oil with the butter in a large frying pan, add the fish and fry for 5 to 6 minutes on each side until cooked and golden.

Transfer to a shallow flameproof dish and top with the vegetable mixture. Sprinkle with cheese and place under a preheated moderate grill until lightly browned. Serve immediately.

Serves 4

VARIATION: Plaice fillets can be used instead of sole.

PLAICE WITH SMOKED SALMON IN LEMON SAUCE

2 plaice, filleted and skinned
50 g (2 oz) smoked salmon, in 2 slices
250 g (8 oz) frozen chopped spinach, thawed
WHITE SAUCE:
15 g ($\frac{1}{2}$ oz) butter
15 g ($\frac{1}{2}$ oz) plain flour
150 ml ($\frac{1}{4}$ pint) milk
2 tablespoons lemon juice
salt and pepper
TO GARNISH:
lemon wedges
parsley sprigs

Take 2 plaice fillets and lay a piece of smoked salmon on top of each. Place the remaining fillets on top.

Place the spinach in a buttered ovenproof dish, large enough to hold the plaice side by side. Arrange the fish on top of the spinach.

Make the white sauce: melt the butter in a pan, stir in the flour and cook for 1 minute. Gradually stir in the milk and bring to the boil. Stir in the lemon juice, and salt and pepper to taste. Pour over the fish.

Cook in a preheated moderate oven, 180°C (350°F), Gas Mark 4, for 10 to 15 minutes. Garnish with lemon wedges and parsley to serve.

Serves 2

RED MULLET WITH CHICORY

350 g (12 oz) chicory
25 g (1 oz) unsalted butter
2 small onions, sliced
2 teaspoons lemon juice
salt and pepper
4 small red mullet, cleaned and scaled
TO GARNISH:
dill sprigs
lemon wedges

Blanch the chicory in boiling salted water for 5 minutes. Drain, then break off and slice the leaves.

Melt the butter in a pan, stir in the onion, chicory, lemon juice, and salt and pepper to taste. Cover and cook for 5 minutes.

Spoon the chicory mixture into an ovenproof dish. Place the red mullet on top and sprinkle with salt and pepper. Cover with foil and cook in a preheated moderate oven, 180°C (350°F), Gas Mark 4, for 20 minutes or until cooked. Garnish with dill and lemon to serve.

Serves 4

VARIATION: Replace the chicory with sliced fennel.

TAGLIATELLE WITH SMOKED BUCKLING

250 g (8 oz) dried tagliatelle verdi
1 tablespoon sunflower oil
50 g (2 oz) mushrooms, sliced
250 g (8 oz) cream cheese with garlic and herbs
350 g (12 oz) smoked buckling, skinned, boned and flaked
1 tablespoon chopped parsley to garnish

Cook the tagliatelle according to the packet directions.

Meanwhile, heat the oil in a large pan, add the mushrooms and sauté for 3 minutes. Add the cheese and heat gently until melted; be careful not to boil.

Drain the tagliatelle, add to the pan, then stir in the fish.

Garnish with the parsley and serve immediately.

Serves 4

VARIATION: Use smoked trout instead of smoked buckling.

HALIBUT WITH RHUBARB

250 g (8 oz) rhubarb, cut into 1 cm (½ inch) pieces
1 tablespoon soft brown sugar
1 tablespoon chopped mint
5 tablespoons dry white wine
2 halibut steaks
salt and pepper
mint sprigs to garnish

Put the rhubarb, sugar and mint into a casserole, then pour over the wine. Place the fish on top, and season with salt and pepper to taste.

Cover and cook in a preheated moderately hot oven, 200°C (400°F), Gas Mark 6, for 15 to 20 minutes, until tender.

Garnish with mint and serve immediately, with creamed potatoes.

Serves 2

LEFT: *Plaice with Smoked Salmon in Lemon Sauce; Red Mullet with Chicory*
RIGHT: *Stir-Fried Fish with Vegetables*

STIR-FRIED FISH WITH VEGETABLES

500 g (1 lb) cod fillet, skinned and cut into 2.5 cm (1 inch) wide strips
1 teaspoon salt
1 tablespoon oil
2 rashers back bacon, derinded and shredded
50 g (2 oz) frozen peas, cooked
50 g (2 oz) frozen sweetcorn, cooked
6 tablespoons chicken stock or water
2 teaspoons Chinese wine or dry sherry
2 teaspoons soy sauce
1 teaspoon sugar
1 teaspoon cornflour
1 teaspoon water
spring onion tassels to garnish (see right)

Sprinkle the fish strips with the salt and leave for 15 minutes.

Heat the oil in a frying pan, add the fish and bacon and stir-fry for 3 minutes. Add the remaining ingredients, except the cornflour and water, and bring to the boil. Blend the cornflour with the water and stir into the pan. Cook for 1 minute.

Garnish with spring onion tassels and serve immediately.

Serves 4

TO MAKE SPRING ONION TASSELS: Trim the tops off the spring onions and remove the root base. Shred carefully, leaving 2.5 cm (1 inch) attached. Immerse in iced water until the spring onions open out and curl.

SKATE PARCELS

3 tablespoons sunflower oil
2 carrots, sliced into matchstick pieces
3 celery sticks, sliced lengthways
½ fennel bulb, sliced lengthways
8 spring onions, sliced lengthways
1 courgette, sliced lengthways
1 tablespoon soy sauce
1 tablespoon dry sherry
1 tablespoon tomato ketchup
salt and pepper
4 skate wings
orange twists to garnish

Heat 1 tablespoon of the oil in a frying pan, add the vegetables and stir-fry for 3 minutes.

Add the soy sauce, sherry, tomato ketchup, and salt and pepper to taste and simmer for 2 minutes. Set aside.

Heat the remaining oil in another pan, add the skate wings and fry quickly for 2 minutes on each side.

Place each skate wing on a large piece of foil and cover with the vegetable mixture. Fold the foil over to form a parcel and seal well.

Place on a baking sheet and cook in a preheated moderately hot oven, 200°C (400°F), Gas Mark 6, for 15 to 20 minutes, until tender.

Garnish with orange twists and serve immediately.

Serves 4

PRAWNS IN GINGER SAUCE

8 spring onions, chopped
5 cm (2 inch) piece fresh root ginger, chopped
2 tablespoons dry sherry
2 tablespoons soy sauce
150 ml (¼ pint) chicken stock
salt and pepper
12 Mediterranean prawns, peeled

Put all the ingredients, except the prawns, into a saucepan, seasoning with salt and pepper to taste. Bring to the boil, then simmer for 2 minutes. Stir in the prawns, cover and cook for 3 minutes. Serve immediately, with rice or noodles.

Serves 4

Prawns in Ginger Sauce

RED MULLET IN VINE LEAVES

6 vine leaves
2 × 250 g (8 oz) red mullet, scaled and washed
sunflower oil for brushing
STUFFING:
1 large tomato, chopped
2 anchovy fillets, chopped
2 tablespoons chopped parsley
1 tablespoon chopped basil
1 clove garlic, crushed
salt and pepper
TO GARNISH:
4 anchovies
2 black olives

Mix the stuffing ingredients together, seasoning with salt and pepper, and divide between 2 vine leaves, spreading over one side of each leaf.

Arrange the vine leaves overlapping in two groups of three, with a covered vine leaf forming the centre of each group. Place the mullet on top and wrap the vine leaves around.

Place in a roasting pan, brush with oil and cook in a preheated moderately hot oven, 200°C (400°F), Gas Mark 6, for 15 minutes.

Transfer to a warmed serving dish and top with the anchovies and olives.

Serves 2

(Picture, page 46)

WHOLEWHEAT FISH CRUMBLE

750 g ($1\frac{1}{2}$ lb) halibut
300 ml ($\frac{1}{2}$ pint) milk
1 bouquet garni
salt and pepper
1 celery heart, cut into 1 cm ($\frac{1}{2}$ inch) pieces
1 small fennel bulb, diced
2 leeks, sliced
1 carrot, sliced
1 teaspoon grated lemon rind
1 tablespoon lemon juice
150 ml ($\frac{1}{4}$ pint) water
40 g ($1\frac{1}{2}$ oz) unsalted butter
40 g ($1\frac{1}{2}$ oz) plain flour
3 tablespoons fromage frais or Greek yogurt
2 tablespoons chopped parsley
1 teaspoon chopped fennel leaves

TOPPING:
50 g (2 oz) unsalted butter
125 g (4 oz) wholewheat flour
75 g (3 oz) matured Cheddar cheese, grated
$\frac{1}{2}$ teaspoon chilli powder

Put the fish into a saucepan with the milk, bouquet garni, and salt and pepper to taste, cover and simmer for 10 to 15 minutes, until the fish flakes away from the skin. Remove with a slotted spoon, reserving the cooking liquid. Remove any skin and bones and flake the fish into large pieces.

Put the vegetables into a saucepan with the lemon rind, juice and water. Bring to the boil, then cover and simmer for 5 minutes, until just tender. Drain, reserving the cooking liquid, and set aside.

Melt the butter in a pan, stir in the flour and cook for 1 minute. Gradually stir in the reserved cooking liquids, bring to the boil and boil for 1 minute. Remove from the heat and stir in the fromage frais or Greek yogurt, parsley, fennel leaves, fish and vegetables. Pour into a 1.2 litre (2 pint) pie dish.

Rub the butter into the flour until the mixture resembles breadcrumbs. Stir in the cheese and chilli powder and sprinkle over the fish mixture.

Cook in a preheated moderately hot oven, 200°C (400°F), Gas Mark 6, for 20 minutes. Serve hot.

Serves 4 to 6

QUICK-FRY SALMON

1 tablespoon sunflower oil
1 onion, chopped
500 g (1 lb) potatoes, parboiled and diced
1 × 439 g ($15\frac{1}{2}$ oz) can salmon, drained and flaked
2 tablespoons chopped parsley
125 g (4 oz) frozen peas
pepper
parsley sprigs to garnish

Heat the oil in a pan, add the onion and sauté until soft and transparent.

Add the potatoes and fry for 5 minutes, stirring.

Stir in the salmon, parsley, peas, and pepper to taste. Fry gently for 5 minutes, until heated through. Garnish with parsley and serve immediately.

Serves 4

Quick-Fry Salmon

Sardine Pizza

COUNTRY TROUT

2 tablespoons lemon or lime juice
1 tablespoon chopped parsley
1 tablespoon chopped thyme
1 tablespoon chopped chives
1 shallot or small onion, very finely chopped
25 g (1 oz) butter, softened
salt and pepper
4 rainbow trout, cleaned
4 rashers streaky bacon, derinded
4 lemon or lime slices
4 rosemary sprigs

Mix together the lemon or lime juice, herbs, shallot or small onion, butter and salt and pepper to taste. Divide the mixture into 4 portions and spread into the cavities of the trout. Secure with cocktail sticks or sew up.

Wrap a rasher of bacon around each trout. Place each fish on a piece of foil, top with a lemon or lime slice and a rosemary sprig and wrap securely in the foil. Cook under a preheated moderate grill, or on a barbecue grid 10 cm (4 inches) above the coals, for 10 minutes each side.

Serve in the foil, with jacket potatoes and a green salad.

Serves 4

SARDINE PIZZA

1 × 150 g (6 oz) packet pizza base mix
1 × 120 g (4 oz) can sardines in oil, drained and mashed
1 × 397 g (14 oz) can tomatoes, drained and chopped
½ teaspoon chopped oregano
salt and pepper
1 green pepper, cored, seeded and sliced
50 g (2 oz) mushrooms, sliced
125 g (4 oz) Mozzarella cheese, sliced
1 × 50 g (1¾ oz) can anchovy fillets, drained
6 black olives

Make up the pizza mix according to packet directions. Roll into an 18 cm (7 inch) circle and place on a baking sheet.

Put the sardines, tomatoes, oregano, and salt and pepper to taste into a bowl and mix well to combine. Spoon onto the pizza base and arrange the green pepper and mushrooms attractively on top. Cover with the cheese slices.

Arrange the anchovies in a criss-cross pattern on top and finish with the olives.

Cook in a preheated moderately hot oven, 200°C (400°F), Gas Mark 6, for 20 to 25 minutes.

Serve immediately, with a green salad.

Serves 4 to 6

VARIATION: Replace the sardines with 1 × 99 g (3½ oz) can tuna steak.

HADDOCK AND EGG MORNAY

4 smoked haddock fillets, skinned
450 ml (¾ pint) milk
1 bouquet garni
4 eggs
40 g (1½ oz) butter
40 g (1½ oz) plain flour
75 g (3 oz) Cheddar cheese
pepper
parsley sprigs to garnish

Put the haddock into a pan with the milk and bouquet garni. Cook over low heat for 10 minutes or until tender. Transfer to a warmed serving dish, using a slotted spoon, and keep hot. Strain the milk and reserve.

Poach the eggs in simmering water for 4 to 5 minutes. Meanwhile, melt the butter in a pan. Stir in the flour and cook, stirring, for 2 minutes. Blend in the milk and simmer, stirring, until thickened. Stir in two-thirds of the cheese.

Using a slotted spoon, place a poached egg on each haddock fillet. Top with the cheese sauce and sprinkle with the remaining Cheddar cheese and add pepper to taste. Place under a preheated hot grill until lightly browned. Serve immediately, garnished with sprigs of parsley.

Serves 4

MARINER'S PIE

450 ml ($\frac{3}{4}$ pint) milk
1 bay leaf
2 lemon slices
salt and pepper
500 g (1 lb) whiting fillets
50 g (2 oz) butter
125 g (4 oz) button mushrooms, quartered
40 g ($1\frac{1}{2}$ oz) plain flour
3 tablespoons natural low-fat yogurt or soured cream
2 tablespoons chopped parsley
2 hard-boiled eggs, chopped
500 g (1 lb) potatoes, boiled and sliced
50 g (2 oz) Cheddar cheese, grated
parsley sprigs to garnish

Put the milk, bay leaf, lemon slices, and salt and pepper to taste into a saucepan and bring to the boil. Add the fish and simmer for 10 to 15 minutes, until tender. Remove with a slotted spoon. Strain and reserve the liquid. Flake the fish, removing any skin or bones.

Melt the butter in a pan, add the mushrooms and cook for 2 minutes. Stir in the flour, cook for 1 minute, then gradually stir in the reserved liquid and bring to the boil.

Remove from the heat and stir in the fish, yogurt or soured cream, parsley and chopped eggs. Check the seasoning and pour into a 1.2 litre (2 pint) pie dish. Arrange the potato on top, then sprinkle with the cheese.

Cook under a preheated moderate grill for 5 minutes, or in a preheated moderate oven, 180°C (350°F), Gas Mark 4, for 10 to 15 minutes.

Garnish with the parsley and serve immediately.

Serves 4

CREAMED COCONUT MONKFISH

125 g (4 oz) desiccated coconut
300 ml ($\frac{1}{2}$ pint) boiling water
1 tablespoon oil
6 spring onions, chopped
3 green chillies, seeded and chopped
1 red pepper, cored, seeded and chopped
1 clove garlic, crushed
5 cm (2 inch) piece fresh root ginger, chopped
$\frac{1}{2}$ teaspoon ground cumin
$\frac{1}{2}$ teaspoon ground coriander
1 teaspoon grated lemon rind
1 tablespoon lime juice
1 tablespoon sherry
salt and pepper
750 g ($1\frac{1}{2}$ lb) monkfish, cut into 5 cm (2 inch) cubes
TO GARNISH:
lime wedges
coriander leaves

Put the coconut into a bowl, pour over the boiling water and leave to infuse for 30 minutes. Strain and reserve the liquid, discarding the coconut.

Heat the oil in a large pan and stir in the remaining ingredients, except the fish, seasoning with salt and pepper to taste. Add the fish, pour on the coconut milk and bring to the boil, then simmer for 5 minutes.

Transfer to a warmed serving dish, garnish with lime and coriander, and serve with rice.

Serves 4

Mariner's Pie; Creamed Coconut Monkfish

SALMON SAVOURY

2 × 213 g ($7\frac{1}{2}$ oz) cans salmon, drained and mashed
250 g (8 oz) Cheddar cheese, grated
4 tablespoons natural low-fat yogurt
4 tablespoons lemon juice
salt and pepper
paprika
4 eggs, beaten
4 slices wholemeal bread, toasted and buttered
lemon wedges to garnish

Mix the salmon with the cheese. Stir in the yogurt and lemon juice. Season with salt, pepper and paprika to taste. Beat until well mixed, then beat in the eggs.

Put the toast in a shallow flameproof dish and pile the salmon mixture on top. Place under a preheated low grill for 10 minutes or until the mixture is heated through, then increase the heat and grill for a further 5 minutes to brown the top. Serve immediately, with lemon wedges.

Serves 4

CARIBBEAN SCAMPI

350 g (12 oz) uncooked scampi
3 tablespoons plain flour
oil for deep-frying
50 g (2 oz) desiccated coconut
BATTER:
125 g (4 oz) plain flour
pinch of salt
2 teaspoons sunflower oil
7–8 tablespoons beer or tepid water
2 egg whites
TO GARNISH:
coriander sprig
lime wedges

First, make the batter. Sift the flour and salt into a bowl, then beat in the oil and beer or water to form a smooth thick batter.

Just before using, whisk the egg whites until soft peaks form, then gently fold into the batter mixture.

Toss the scampi in the flour, then dip into the batter to coat thickly and evenly.

Deep-fry a few at a time in the hot oil for 5 to 7 minutes, until crisp and golden. Drain on kitchen paper, then toss in the coconut.

Serve immediately, garnished with coriander and lime.

Serves 4

GRILLED SOLE WITH PRAWN SAUCE

4 sole fillets
juice of 1 lemon
25 g (1 oz) butter
SAUCE:
250 g (8 oz) peeled prawns
finely grated rind and juice of 1 lemon
1 tablespoon chopped parsley
1 tablespoon chopped chives
salt and pepper
TO GARNISH:
few cooked whole prawns
lemon slices

Sprinkle the fish with the lemon juice, dot with the fat and cook under a preheated medium grill for 2 to 3 minutes on each side.

Meanwhile, prepare the sauce. Put the prawns, lemon rind and juice, herbs, and salt and pepper to taste into a pan and heat gently.

Roll up the sole fillets and arrange on serving plates. Spoon over the prawn sauce. Garnish with whole prawns and lemon slices and serve immediately.

Serves 4

Caribbean Scampi

SOLE FILLETS WITH COURGETTES

50 g (2 oz) unsalted butter
350 g (12 oz) small courgettes, thinly sliced
salt and pepper
1 large tomato, skinned, seeded and chopped
4 Dover sole fillets
2 tablespoons lemon juice
1 tablespoon chopped basil
1 tablespoon fresh breadcrumbs
basil leaves to garnish

Melt half the butter in a pan, add the courgettes, and salt and pepper to taste and sauté for 3 minutes.

Add the tomato and continue cooking for 3 minutes, stirring occasionally.

Place the sole fillets in a gratin dish, dot with the remaining butter, and season with salt and pepper to taste. Pour over the lemon juice and sprinkle with the basil.

Pour the tomato and courgette mixture evenly over the fish and sprinkle with the breadcrumbs. Cook in a preheated moderately hot oven, 200°C (400°F), Gas Mark 6, for 10 to 15 minutes, until the fish is tender and the breadcrumbs crisp and golden.

Garnish with basil to serve.

Serves 2

BRILL WITH PEARS

4 brill or small turbot fillets
1 × 212 g ($7\frac{1}{2}$ oz) can pear quarters in natural juice, drained
1 egg yolk
2 tablespoons chopped tarragon
1 tablespoon chopped parsley
1 teaspoon grated lemon rind
salt and pepper
1 × 142 ml (5 fl oz) carton single cream

Wrap one fish fillet around each pear quarter. Place in a buttered ovenproof dish, just large enough to hold the fillets.

Beat the egg yolk, herbs, lemon rind, and salt and pepper to taste into the cream. Pour over the fish.

Cover with foil and cook in a preheated moderate oven, 180°C (350°F), Gas Mark 4, for 25 minutes or until tender. Serve hot.

Serves 4

John Dory Fillets

JOHN DORY FILLETS

25 g (1 oz) plain flour
salt and pepper
6 John Dory fillets
175 g (6 oz) butter
350 g (12 oz) mushrooms, sliced
1 clove garlic, crushed
8 tablespoons double cream
1 teaspoon lemon juice
TO GARNISH:
parsley sprigs
lemon wedges

Season the flour with salt and pepper and use to coat the fish.

Heat 125 g (4 oz) of the butter in a small pan until bubbling. Line a sieve with muslin and pour the butter through this into a frying pan. Add the fish and fry gently for 3 minutes on each side. Keep warm.

Melt the remaining butter in another pan, add the mushrooms and garlic, cover and simmer for 8 minutes. Stir in the cream, lemon juice, and salt and pepper to taste and heat gently.

Arrange the fish on a warmed serving dish and pour over the sauce. Garnish with parsley and lemon wedges to serve.

Serves 6

SEAFOOD CURRY

2 tablespoons oil
2 onions, chopped
½ red pepper, cored, seeded and chopped
2 celery sticks, chopped
50 g (2 oz) mushrooms, sliced
1½ tablespoons curry powder
½ teaspoon turmeric
½ teaspoon ground ginger
1 cooking apple, peeled, cored and diced
250 g (8 oz) haddock fillet
125 g (4 oz) prawns
50 g (2 oz) raisins
1 teaspoon Worcestershire sauce
2 teaspoons tomato purée
6 tablespoons white wine
6 tablespoons water
salt and pepper
2 tablespoons natural low-fat yogurt
juice of ½ lemon

Heat the oil in a large pan. Add the onions, pepper, celery and mushrooms and fry gently for 5 minutes. Add the curry powder, turmeric and ginger and cook, stirring, for 2 minutes.

Add the apple, haddock, prawns, raisins, Worcestershire sauce and tomato purée and stir well. Stir in the wine and water and season with salt and pepper to taste. Cover and simmer gently for 10 minutes.

Just before serving, stir in the yogurt and lemon juice. Serve with plain boiled rice.

Serves 4

FISH WITH GREEN MAYONNAISE

500 g (1 lb) cod fillets
150 ml (¼ pint) dry white wine
bouquet garni
salt and pepper
250 g (8 oz) peeled prawns
250 g (8 oz) spinach
1 clove garlic
4 spring onions
1 tablespoon oil
1 tablespoon lemon juice
6 tablespoons Mayonnaise (see page 21)
4 tablespoons double cream
TO GARNISH:
mustard and cress
lemon slices

Put the cod into a shallow frying pan, pour over the wine, add the bouquet garni, and season well with salt and pepper. Bring to the boil and simmer for 7 to 10 minutes, until cooked. Drain and flake the fish. Mix with the prawns.

Put the spinach, garlic and spring onions into a blender or food processor and work until smooth. Add the oil, lemon juice, Mayonnaise and cream and blend again. The mixture should be like thick mayonnaise; if it is too thick add a little more cream or lemon juice to taste. Fold in the fish.

Transfer to individual serving dishes and sprinkle with the mustard and cress. Garnish with lemon slices to serve.

Serves 4

CRISPY TOP COD

300 ml (½ pint) boiling water
1 bouquet garni
1 onion, roughly chopped
4 chunky cod fillets
2×25 g (1 oz) packets ready salted crisps, crushed
CHEESE SAUCE:
40 g (1½ oz) butter
40 g (1½ oz) plain flour
450 ml (¾ pint) milk
salt and pepper
75 g (3 oz) Cheddar cheese, grated
TO GARNISH:
parsley sprigs
lemon twists

Put the water, bouquet garni and onion into a large pan, add the cod and cook for 10 to 15 minutes, until tender.

Meanwhile, make the cheese sauce: melt the butter in a pan then stir in the flour. Cook, stirring, for 1 to 2 minutes. Remove from the heat and gradually stir in the milk. Return to the heat and bring to the boil stirring. Season with salt and pepper to taste and stir in the cheese. Set aside.

Remove the fish with a slotted spoon and place in a shallow dish.

Pour the sauce over the fish. Sprinkle the crisps over.

Cook under a preheated hot grill for 2 to 3 minutes, until golden. Garnish with parsley and lemon and serve immediately.

Serves 4 to 6

BAKED TROUT

50 g (2 oz) butter
4 trout, cleaned
1 lemon, sliced
5 tablespoons dry white wine
1 teaspoon dried tarragon
salt and pepper
parsley sprigs to garnish

Line a baking dish with a large piece of foil, allowing sufficient to hang over the sides. Spread the butter over the foil. Lay the trout in the dish and arrange the lemon slices on top.

Mix together the wine, tarragon and salt and pepper to taste and pour over the fish.

Fold the foil over the trout to make a parcel and fold the edges together to seal. Cook in a preheated moderate oven, 180°C (350°F), Gas Mark 4, for 30 minutes.

Transfer the trout to a warmed serving dish. Pour over the juices and garnish with parsley.

Serves 4

PACIFIC TUNA PIE

2 × 198 g (7 oz) cans tuna steak, drained and flaked
1 × 326 g ($11\frac{1}{2}$ oz) can sweetcorn, drained
1 × 113 g (4 oz) packet frozen peas
1 × 298 g ($10\frac{1}{2}$ oz) can condensed chicken soup
1 × 397 g (14 oz) can tomatoes, drained
75 g (3 oz) Cheddar cheese, grated
1 × 75 g (3 oz) packet potato crisps, crushed

Mix together the tuna, sweetcorn, peas and soup. Turn into a buttered casserole and cover with the tomatoes.

Mix together the cheese and crisps and sprinkle over the tomatoes. Cook in a preheated moderately hot oven, 190°C (375°F), Gas Mark 5, for 30 minutes, until the top is golden and bubbling.

Serve hot, with baked tomatoes if liked.

Serves 4

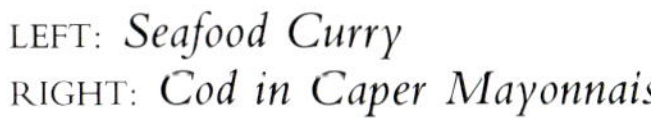

LEFT: *Seafood Curry*
RIGHT: *Cod in Caper Mayonnaise*

COD IN CAPER MAYONNAISE

4 cod fillets, skinned
salt and pepper
150 ml ($\frac{1}{4}$ pint) dry white wine
$\frac{1}{2}$ lemon, sliced
6 tablespoons Mayonnaise (see page 21)
4 tablespoons lemon juice
50 g (2 oz) capers, chopped

Put the cod fillets into a frying pan and sprinkle them with salt and pepper to taste. Add the dry white wine and lemon slices, cover and simmer for 20 minutes.

Remove the fish from the pan, reserving 2 tablespoons of the cooking liquor, and leave to cool.

Mix together the Mayonnaise, lemon juice and the reserved liquor. Stir in the capers.

Place the fish in a serving dish and top with the caper sauce. This dish is served cold.

Serves 4

PLAICE IN ORANGE MAYONNAISE

4 plaice, skinned and filleted
grated rind and juice of 2 oranges
juice of 1 lemon
salt and pepper
150 ml (¼ pint) Mayonnaise (see page 21)
TO GARNISH:
anchovy fillets
orange segments

Sprinkle the fish with the rind and juice of 1 orange, the lemon juice, and salt and pepper to taste. Roll up and place in a buttered ovenproof dish. Cover and cook in a preheated moderate oven, 180°C (350°F), Gas Mark 4, for 20 minutes or until just tender. Leave to cool.

Add the remaining grated orange rind and juice to the Mayonnaise and mix well.

Place the fish in a serving dish and pour over the flavoured mayonnaise. Garnish with anchovy fillets and orange segments. Serve cold.

Serves 4

TUNA AND BEAN SALAD

1 × 99 g (3½ oz) and 1 × 198 g (7 oz) can tuna steak, drained and flaked
1 × 439 g (15½ oz) can butter beans, drained
4 tablespoons French Dressing (see page 15)
chopped capers to garnish

Mix the tuna and butter beans together. Pour over the French dressing and toss well to coat.

Turn into a serving dish and garnish with capers.

Serves 4

CRUNCHY SALMON SALAD

3 tablespoons Mayonnaise (see page 21)
6 tablespoons lemon juice
2 × 213 g (7½ oz) cans red salmon, drained and flaked
2 dessert apples, cored and diced
175 g (6 oz) salted peanuts, chopped
salt and pepper
1 lettuce

Mix the Mayonnaise and lemon juice together in a bowl. Add the salmon and stir in the apples, peanuts and salt and pepper to taste.

Line a serving dish with lettuce leaves and pile the salmon mixture into the centre.

Serves 4

LEFT: *Plaice in Orange Mayonnaise; Crunchy Salmon Salad*
RIGHT: *Quick Paella; Italian Risotto with Prawns*

QUICK PAELLA

4 small squid, heads and ink sacs removed
2 tablespoons oil
3 cloves garlic, sliced
50 g (2 oz) streaky bacon, derinded and diced
250 g (8 oz) long-grain rice
4 tomatoes, skinned, seeded and chopped
150 ml (¼ pint) dry white wine
150 ml (¼ pint) chicken stock
salt and pepper
1 red pepper, cored, seeded and chopped
125 g (4 oz) chorizo or garlic sausage, sliced
few saffron strands
1 × 397 g (14 oz) can artichokes, drained and quartered
12 canned mussels, drained
125 g (4 oz) peeled prawns
lemon slices to garnish

Slice the squid and set aside. Heat the oil in a large frying pan, add the garlic and cook, without browning. Add the bacon and cook for 5 minutes.

Add the rice, tomatoes, wine, stock, and salt and pepper to taste. Bring to the boil, simmer for 5 minutes, then add the red pepper, sausage, saffron and squid. Cook for 10 to 12 minutes, until the rice is tender.

Add the artichokes to the pan with the mussels and prawns and cook for 5 minutes.

Garnish with the lemon slices and serve immediately.

Serves 4 to 6

ITALIAN RISOTTO WITH PRAWNS

4 dried cêpes, or 50 g (2 oz) flat open mushrooms
1 tablespoon oil
15 g (½ oz) butter
2 cloves garlic, finely sliced
1 large onion, finely chopped
175 g (6 oz) Italian or short-grain rice
juice of ½ lemon
good pinch of chopped thyme
1 tablespoon chopped parsley
salt and pepper
300 ml (½ pint) dry white wine
300 ml (½ pint) fish or chicken stock
1 tablespoon tomato purée
250 g (8 oz) peeled prawns
4 cooked whole prawns to garnish

Soak the cêpes, if using, in warm water for 15 minutes; squeeze dry. Slice the cêpes or mushrooms.

Heat the oil and butter in a pan, add the garlic and onion and sauté until browned. Add the cêpes or mushrooms, stir in the rice and cook for 1 minute.

Add the lemon juice, herbs and salt and pepper to taste; mix well. Pour over the wine and stock. Bring to the boil and cook, uncovered, for 12 to 15 minutes, until the rice is firm but not over-cooked.

Stir in the tomato purée and increase the heat to reduce any excess liquid. Stir in the prawns. Garnish with whole prawns and serve immediately.

Serves 4

SMOKED HADDOCK SOUFFLÉ OMELETTE

50 g (2 oz) butter
2 smoked haddock fillets, cooked and flaked
5 tablespoons single cream
4 tablespoons grated Parmesan cheese
salt and pepper
6 eggs, separated
parsley sprigs to garnish

Melt half the butter in a saucepan. Add the haddock, cream and half the cheese and heat gently until the cheese is melted.

Remove from the heat and season with salt and pepper. Stir in the egg yolks. Whisk the egg whites until stiff and fold into the haddock mixture.

Melt the remaining butter in a large pan. When sizzling, pour in the omelette mixture. Cook gently for 2 to 3 minutes until set, drawing the cooked edges towards the centre with a fork.

Cut into quarters and turn out onto warmed serving plates. Sprinkle with the remaining cheese and garnish with parsley. Serve immediately.

Serves 4

SPICY SEAFOOD

15 g ($\frac{1}{2}$ oz) butter
2 shallots, chopped
150 ml ($\frac{1}{4}$ pint) dry white wine
2 tablespoons dry sherry
1 teaspoon French mustard
pinch of cayenne
dash of Worcestershire sauce
1 × 142 ml (5 fl oz) carton double cream
2 × 177 g (6 oz) cans crabmeat, drained
250 g (8 oz) peeled prawns
salt and pepper
2–3 tablespoons grated Parmesan cheese
TO GARNISH:
lime slices

Melt the butter in a pan, add the shallots and cook until softened, without browning. Pour in the wine and sherry, bring to the boil and boil rapidly until thickened and reduced by half.

Stir in the mustard, cayenne and Worcestershire sauce and cook for 2 minutes. Add the cream, bring to the boil, and boil for 5 to 7 minutes, stirring occasionally, until thickened.

Remove from the heat, stir in the fish and season with salt and pepper to taste.

Sprinkle with the cheese and serve immediately. Garnish with lime slices and serve rice or new potatoes and a tossed mixed salad as accompaniments.

Serves 4

CREOLE-STYLE PRAWNS

1 tablespoon oil
1 large onion, chopped
1 clove garlic, crushed
2 celery sticks, thinly sliced
350 g (12 oz) tomatoes, skinned, seeded and chopped
1 green pepper, cored, seeded and finely chopped
salt and pepper
4 tablespoons dry white wine
1 tablespoon tomato purée
500 g (1 lb) peeled prawns
2 drops Tabasco sauce
1 teaspoon Worcestershire sauce
1 tablespoon chopped parsley
TO GARNISH:
lemon twists
celery leaves (optional)

Heat the oil in a pan, add the onion and garlic and fry until lightly browned. Add the celery and cook for 2 minutes.

Add the tomatoes and pepper to the pan with salt and pepper to taste. Stir in the wine and tomato purée. Bring to the boil and simmer, uncovered, for 20 minutes.

Stir in the prawns, Tabasco and Worcestershire sauces. Simmer for 5 minutes, then stir in the parsley. Serve immediately, garnished with lemon twists and celery leaves, if liked. Serve with rice or pasta and a green salad.

Serves 6

SPEEDY MAYONNAISE

If you have an electric blender, then you can make Mayonnaise very quickly. To make 300 ml ($\frac{1}{2}$ pint) Mayonnaise, place 1 egg, $\frac{1}{2}$ teaspoon each of salt, pepper and mustard powder and 2 teaspoons of wine vinegar in the bowl and blend on medium speed for a few seconds. Still on medium speed, add 150 ml ($\frac{1}{4}$ pint) each of olive and sunflower oil through the lid. Begin by adding the oil, drop by drop, then as the mixture thickens, pour it into the blender in a thin stream. This Mayonnaise can be kept in the refrigerator in an airtight container for up to 10 days.

Creole-Style Prawns

FISH CASSEROLE WITH PEPPERS

1 tablespoon oil
3 spring onions, chopped, including green part
1 green pepper, cored, seeded and cut into strips
1 red pepper, cored, seeded and cut into strips
1 × 397 g (14 oz) can chopped tomatoes
½ teaspoon sugar
4–6 frozen cod fillets, thawed
juice of 1 lemon
pepper
1 heaped tablespoon chopped parsley

Heat the oil in a flameproof casserole, add the spring onions and fry for about 1 minute, stirring, without browning. Add the peppers and stir-fry for about 3 minutes.

Add the tomatoes, with their juice, and sugar and bring to the boil. Simmer for 5 minutes, then lay the cod on top. Squeeze over the lemon juice; season with pepper to taste and sprinkle with the parsley.

Cover and cook in a preheated moderate oven, 180°C (350°F), Gas Mark 4, for 15 to 20 minutes, depending on the thickness of the fillets.

Serve each portion of fish with some of the pepper mixture and accompany with wholewheat rolls.

Serves 4 to 6

BAKED FISH WITH LIMES

4–6 haddock fillets, fresh or frozen and thawed
finely grated rind and juice of 1 lime
pepper
15–25 g (½–1 oz) butter, melted
TO GARNISH:
watercress sprigs
lime slices

Put the fish into a lightly greased, shallow ovenproof dish. Sprinkle with the lime rind and season with pepper to taste. Pour the lime juice over the fillets and brush a little butter on each.

Bake above the centre of a preheated moderately hot oven, 190°C (375°F), Gas Mark 5, for about 15 to 20 minutes, depending on the thickness of the fillets.

Garnish each fillet with watercress and lime slices.

Serve with rice, green beans, broccoli or peas, grilled tomatoes and wholewheat rolls or crusty French bread.

Serves 4 to 6

Fish Casserole with Peppers; Baked Fish with Limes

PLAICE WITH CUCUMBER

4 plaice fillets, fresh or frozen and thawed
25 g (1 oz) butter, melted
pepper
1 tablespoon oil
2 spring onions, chopped, including green part
50 g (2 oz) mushrooms, thinly sliced
½ cucumber, quartered lengthways then thinly sliced
juice of 1 lemon
lemon wedges to garnish

Lay the fish in a greased grill pan, brush lightly with the melted butter and season with pepper to taste. Cook under a preheated moderate grill for 3 to 4 minutes, turning the fish once.

Heat the oil in a frying pan, add the spring onions and fry for 30 seconds, stirring, without browning. Add the mushrooms and stir-fry for 1 minute. Add the cucumber and lemon juice and heat through.

Arrange the fish on warmed serving plates and garnish with lemon wedges. Serve with the mushroom mixture, grilled tomatoes and wholewheat bread.

Serves 4

MACKEREL WITH CHERRIES

125–175 g (4–6 oz) red cherries, stoned and chopped
4 tablespoons red wine
4 tablespoons water
sugar
4–6 fresh mackerel, filleted
pepper
TO GARNISH:
lemon twists
parsley or watercress sprigs

Simmer the cherries in the wine and water for 10 minutes, until soft. Add a little sugar to taste, but keep the flavour tart. Cool for 1 minute, then purée in an electric blender or food processor or mash with a fork. Return to the pan and keep warm while cooking the fish.

Meanwhile, season the mackerel with pepper and cook under a preheated low grill for 5 minutes on each side.

Transfer to warmed serving plates and serve immediately with the hot cherry sauce. Garnish with lemon and parsley or watercress. Peas and wholewheat rolls go well with this dish.

VARIATION: If fresh cherries are not available, use a 425 g (15 oz) can red cherries, drained, instead. If they taste too sweet, omit sugar and add 1 to 2 teaspoons lemon juice.

Serves 4 to 6

Plaice with Cucumber; Mackerel with Cherries

MEAT AND POULTRY

If a quick meat or poultry dish conjures up thoughts of a solitary grilled chop, plainly cooked mince or a roast chicken portion, then delve into this chapter for some delightful surprises. Speediness needn't mean sameness as you will see when you sample grilled pork chops with lashings of super cider sauce, made all the tastier with a drop of Calvados; minced beef gently simmered with onions, garlic, chilli, tomatoes and red kidney beans and transformed into a Chilli Con Carne to eat with rice or crusty French bread; or chicken breasts stir-fried with spring onions, walnuts, peppers, courgettes, mushrooms, ginger and mangetout for a Chinese-style feast.

Speedy meat and poultry dishes can also be cheap and cheerful ones if you buy economical cuts of meat and offal like lamb's kidneys, chicken livers, chicken portions and delicatessen offerings like frankfurters and garlic sausage as well as the more costly steaks, veal escalopes and chicken breasts and fillets.

Many recipes rely upon flavour-giving herb and spice butters for extra tastiness and it is worthwhile making batches of versatile garlic, parsley or lemon butter in bulk – they will keep in the refrigerator for up to 2 weeks. Other dishes can be given a luxury touch with a dash of wine, spirit or liqueur, a spoonful of cream, a slice of pâté or sprinkling of peppercorns. A well-stocked storecupboard with grated Parmesan cheese, a variety of nuts, capers, mustards, Worcestershire sauce and dried fruits will pay unlimited dividends when producing imaginative meat and poultry dishes.

STEAK AU POIVRE

2 tablespoons green peppercorns, or 1 tablespoon black peppercorns
4 × 150 g (5 oz) rump or fillet steaks
salt
50 g (2 oz) butter
2 tablespoons brandy
1 × 142 ml (5 fl oz) carton double cream
watercress sprigs to garnish

Crush half the peppercorns and rub into the steaks. Season to taste with salt. Melt the butter in a large frying pan, add the steaks and fry quickly on both sides until browned. Cook for 3 to 5 minutes on each side, according to taste. Pour over the brandy, remove from the heat and ignite; when the flames have died down, arrange the steaks on a warmed serving dish.

Add the cream to the pan and cook, without boiling, for 1 minute. Add the remaining peppercorns. Spoon over the steaks, garnish with watercress and serve immediately.

Serves 4

ABOVE: *Steak au Poivre*
RIGHT: *Côtés de Porc Vallée d'Auge; Veal in Cream and Mushroom Sauce*

TOURNEDOS ROSSINI

50 g (2 oz) butter
125 g (4 oz) button mushrooms, finely chopped
1 × 113 g (4 oz) can pâté de foie, cut into 2.5 cm (1 inch) rounds
4 tablespoons Madeira
salt and pepper
1 × 397 g (14 oz) can artichoke hearts
6 fillet steaks, 2.5 cm (1 inch) thick

(Picture, page 70)

Melt half the butter in a pan, add the mushrooms and fry until golden. Transfer to a heatproof dish with the pâté. Spoon over half the Madeira and season with salt and pepper to taste. Place over a pan of hot water to heat through gently. Heat the artichokes in a small pan, then drain.

Season the steaks with salt and pepper to taste. Melt the remaining butter in a pan, add the steaks and cook for 2 to 4 minutes on each side, according to taste.

Arrange the artichoke hearts and steaks on a warmed serving dish. Spoon over the mushrooms, the liquor and remaining Madeira. Place a slice of pâté on each steak and serve immediately.

Serves 6

ENTRECÔTE À LA MOUTARDE

750 g–1 kg (1½–2 lb) piece sirloin steak, 5 cm (2 inches) thick
3 tablespoons French mustard
salt and pepper
50 g (2 oz) butter
1 × 284 ml (½ pint) carton double cream
3 tablespoons brandy
watercress sprigs to garnish

Spread each side of the steak with 1 tablespoon mustard. Cover and leave for 1 hour. Season to taste with salt and pepper.

Melt the butter in a heavy-based frying pan, add the steak and seal both sides quickly over high heat. Lower the heat and cook for 7 to 12 minutes on each side, according to taste. Place on a warmed dish and keep hot.

Add the remaining mustard and half the cream to the pan, stirring well to incorporate the meat juices. Heat gently. Add the remaining cream and salt and pepper to taste and bring to just below boiling point. Add the brandy and stir well.

Cut the steak into serving portions and pour over the sauce. Garnish with watercress and serve immediately.

Serves 4 to 6

VEAL IN CREAM AND MUSHROOM SAUCE

4 × 125 g (4 oz) veal escalopes, beaten
salt and pepper
25 g (1 oz) butter
1 clove garlic, crushed
250 g (8 oz) mushrooms, sliced
150 ml ($\frac{1}{4}$ pint) Madeira or Marsala
1 × 142 ml (5 fl oz) carton double cream
CROÛTONS:
oil for shallow-frying
3 slices white bread, cut into heart shapes to garnish

Make the croûtons: heat the oil in a frying pan, add the bread and fry until golden brown. Drain on kitchen paper.

Season the veal with salt and pepper to taste. Melt the butter in a large frying pan, add the garlic and mushrooms and fry until soft. Remove and set aside. Add the veal and cook for 3 minutes on each side, until just tender. Pour in the Madeira or Marsala and cook for 3 minutes. Add the cream and mushrooms; simmer until thickened.

Arrange the veal on a warmed serving dish, spoon over the sauce and arrange the croûtons around the edge. Serve hot.

Serves 4

CÔTES DE PORC VALLÉE D'AUGE

4 shallots or small onions, chopped
2 tablespoons chopped parsley
salt and pepper
4 pork chops
25 g (1 oz) butter, melted
150 ml ($\frac{1}{4}$ pint) dry cider
1 tablespoon Calvados (optional)
sage leaves to garnish

Mix the shallots or small onions and parsley together, with salt and pepper to taste. Score the chops on both sides and spread with the mixture. Spoon over a little butter. Cook under a preheated medium grill for about 15 minutes on each side until tender.

Transfer the chops to a frying pan. Drain off any excess fat from the grill pan and pour the juices over the chops. Add the cider and boil for 2 minutes until the liquor has reduced. Stir in the Calvados, if using.

Transfer to a warmed serving dish and garnish with sage.

Serves 4

STUFFED VEAL ROLLS

500 g (1 lb) veal fillet, cut into 8 thin slices
8 thin slices cooked ham or bacon
25 g (1 oz) fresh breadcrumbs, soaked in milk and squeezed dry
3 tablespoons sultanas
25 g (1 oz) pine nuts or blanched slivered almonds
4 tablespoons grated Parmesan cheese
2 tablespoons chopped parsley
salt and pepper
1 tablespoon oil
25 g (1 oz) butter
150 ml ($\frac{1}{4}$ pint) dry white wine
parsley sprigs to garnish

Lay the veal flat between greaseproof paper and beat gently to flatten. Cover each piece of veal with a slice of ham or bacon.

Mix together the breadcrumbs, sultanas, nuts, cheese and parsley, and season with salt and pepper to taste. Divide between the veal slices, roll up and secure each one with a cocktail stick.

Heat the oil and butter in a pan, add the veal rolls and fry until lightly browned. Pour in the wine, cover and cook very gently, turning once, for 20 to 25 minutes until tender.

Transfer the rolls to a warmed serving dish and keep hot. Bring the pan juices to the boil, stirring, and cook until well reduced. Spoon over the meat, garnish with parsley and serve immediately.

Serves 4

Stuffed Veal Rolls

SAUTÉED KIDNEYS

2 tablespoons oil
25 g (1 oz) butter
2 cloves garlic, finely chopped
625 g ($1\frac{1}{4}$ lb) lambs' or calves' kidneys, skinned, halved, cored and thinly sliced
2 tablespoons chopped parsley
1 tablespoon lemon juice
salt and pepper
small triangles of crisp fried bread to garnish

Heat the oil and butter in a large frying pan. Add the garlic and kidneys and fry briskly, stirring constantly, for 2 minutes. Add the parsley, lemon juice, and salt and pepper to taste. Cook, stirring, for 1 to 2 minutes, until the kidneys are tender but juicy.

Serve immediately, garnished with fried bread triangles.

Serves 4

MEAT BALLS IN TOMATO SAUCE

3 slices bread, crusts removed, soaked in milk and squeezed dry
500 g (1 lb) minced veal or beef
2 cloves garlic, crushed
1 tablespoon chopped parsley
1 teaspoon finely grated lemon rind
125 g (4 oz) grated Parmesan cheese
grated nutmeg
salt and pepper
2 eggs, beaten
flour for coating
oil for shallow-frying
300 ml ($\frac{1}{2}$ pint) Tomato Sauce (see right)

Put the bread, meat, garlic, parsley, lemon rind, cheese, and nutmeg, salt and pepper to taste into a bowl. Add the eggs and mix together lightly but thoroughly. Gently shape tablespoonfuls of the mixture into balls, 2.5 cm (1 inch) in diameter. Roll lightly in flour then place in the refrigerator until required.

Pour the oil into a large frying pan to a depth of 5 mm ($\frac{1}{4}$ inch) and place over moderate heat. When the oil is hot, add the meat balls in batches, and fry them for 3 to 4 minutes, turning occasionally, until they are brown on all sides. Lift out and drain on kitchen paper. Pour off the fat, leaving any residue in the pan.

Add the Tomato Sauce to the pan, thinning to a pouring consistency with water if necessary. Return the meat balls to the pan, stir gently and simmer for 15 to 20 minutes until cooked through.

Serves 4

STEAKS WITH GARLIC AND TOMATO SAUCE

4 rump, sirloin, or flash-fry steaks
2 cloves garlic, sliced
olive oil
salt and pepper
Tomato Sauce (see below)
chopped herbs to garnish

Cut small slits in each steak and push in the garlic. Brush the steaks with oil and season with salt and pepper to taste.

Lightly oil the base of a frying pan and place over moderate heat. When hot, add the steaks and fry quickly for 2 minutes on each side.

Spread the steaks with Tomato Sauce, cover the pan and cook over low heat for 5 to 10 minutes, until tender.

Transfer to a warmed serving dish, garnish with herbs and serve immediately.

Serves 4

TOMATO SAUCE

1 × 397 g (14 oz) can peeled tomatoes
1 onion, chopped
1 clove garlic, crushed
1 carrot, sliced
1 celery stick, sliced
2 teaspoons tomato purée
1 teaspoon sugar
salt and pepper
2 teaspoons chopped basil (optional)

Put the tomatoes with their juice, the onion, garlic, carrot, celery, tomato purée and sugar into a saucepan. Add a little salt and pepper and stir with a wooden spoon to break up the tomatoes. Bring to the boil, partially cover and simmer for 30 minutes.

Rub through a sieve and return to the pan. If necessary, boil rapidly, uncovered, until reduced to a sauce consistency. Check the seasoning and stir in the basil, if using.

Serve as required, with pasta or meat dishes.

Makes about 300 ml (½ pint)

Sorrento-Style Pork Slices

SORRENTO-STYLE PORK SLICES

2 tablespoons oil
1 clove garlic, halved
4 boned pork loin chops
salt and pepper
1 large green pepper, cored, seeded and thinly sliced
1 × 227 g (8 oz) can peeled tomatoes
175 g (6 oz) button mushrooms, thinly sliced

Heat the oil and garlic in a large frying pan. When the garlic browns discard it.

Add the chops to the pan and brown lightly on each side. Season with salt and pepper to taste. Cover and cook very gently for 15 minutes. Remove from the pan and keep hot.

Add the pepper and tomatoes, with their juices, to the pan, stirring to break up the tomatoes. Cover and cook gently for 15 minutes.

Stir in the mushrooms and salt and pepper to taste. Cover and cook for 5 minutes.

Return the chops to the pan, baste with the sauce and simmer until heated through. Serve the chops with the sauce spooned over.

Serves 4

Tuscan Grilled Chicken

TURKEY BREAST WITH MARSALA

plain flour for coating
salt and pepper
500 g (1 lb) turkey breast, cut into 4 slices 5 mm (¼ inch) thick
1 tablespoon oil
65 g (2½ oz) butter
125 g (4 oz) button mushrooms, thinly sliced
1 teaspoon lemon juice
2 tablespoons grated Parmesan cheese
4–6 tablespoons Marsala
2 tablespoons chicken stock
cooked broccoli spears to garnish

Season the flour with salt and pepper and use to coat the turkey. Heat the oil and 40 g (1½ oz) of the butter in a large frying pan, add the turkey and fry gently for 4 to 5 minutes on each side, until tender. Transfer to a warmed serving dish and keep hot.

Melt the remaining butter in the pan, add the mushrooms and fry briskly for 3 minutes. Add the lemon juice and a little salt and spread over the turkey slices. Sprinkle with the cheese.

Add the Marsala and stock to the pan and boil rapidly, stirring, until reduced by half. Spoon over the turkey. Garnish with broccoli to serve.

Serves 4

VARIATION: Boned chicken breasts could be used instead of turkey.

TUSCAN GRILLED CHICKEN

1 × 1.25 kg (2½ lb) oven-ready chicken
salt and pepper
MARINADE:
3 tablespoons olive oil
2 tablespoons lemon juice
2 cloves garlic, crushed
6 sage leaves

Halve the chicken along the breast bone and cut out the back bone. Flatten and skewer each wing and leg together. Season liberally with salt and pepper.

Mix the marinade ingredients together in a shallow dish. Add the chicken halves, turning to coat, cover and chill for 4 hours, turning once.

Put the chicken, skin side down, in a grill pan. Cook 13 to 15 cm (5 to 6 inches) below a preheated moderate grill for 12 minutes. Turn and cook for a further 12 minutes or until tender. Baste frequently with the marinade while grilling.

Transfer to a warmed serving dish and pour over the pan juices. Serve with a green salad and crusty bread.

Serves 4

TURKEY BREAST WITH HAM AND CHEESE

plain flour for coating
salt and pepper
500 g (1 lb) boned turkey breast, cut into 4 slices 5 mm (¼ inch) thick
1 egg, beaten
2 tablespoons oil
25 g (1 oz) butter
4 slices cooked ham
150 g (5 oz) Bel Paese or Mozzarella cheese, thinly sliced
parsley sprigs to garnish

Season the flour with salt and pepper. Dip the turkey slices into the egg and then into the seasoned flour. Heat the oil and butter in a large frying pan, add the turkey and fry for about 4 minutes on each side. Drain the turkey slices and transfer them to a grill pan rack.

Cover each portion of turkey with a slice of ham and then with a slice of cheese. Place under a preheated hot grill and cook for 1 minute, until the cheese is golden and bubbling. Serve immediately, garnished with parsley, and a vegetable like green beans or courgettes.

Serves 4

VARIATION: Boned chicken breasts could be used instead of turkey.

CHICKEN WITH ROSEMARY

4 chicken portions
salt and pepper
2 tablespoons oil
25 g (1 oz) butter
2–3 rosemary sprigs
2–3 cloves garlic
6–8 tablespoons dry white wine or chicken stock

Season the chicken with salt and pepper. Heat the oil, butter, rosemary and garlic in a large pan. Add the chicken and fry for 10 to 12 minutes until golden, turning once.

Add the wine or stock and bring to just below boiling point. Simmer, uncovered, for 20 to 30 minutes, until tender. Transfer the chicken to a warmed serving dish and keep hot.

Remove the rosemary and garlic and spoon off the surplus fat from the pan. Add 2 to 4 tablespoons water to the pan juices and bring to the boil, stirring to incorporate the sediment. Pour over the chicken to serve.

Serves 4

CHICKEN BREASTS WITH LEMON

plain flour for coating
salt and pepper
4 boned chicken breasts, halved horizontally
1 tablespoon oil
65 g ($2\frac{1}{2}$ oz) butter
2 tablespoons lemon juice
3 tablespoons chicken stock
3 tablespoons chopped parsley
lemon slices to garnish

Season the flour with salt and pepper and use to coat the chicken pieces.

Heat the oil and 40 g ($1\frac{1}{2}$ oz) of the butter in a large frying pan, add the chicken and fry gently for 5 to 6 minutes on each side until tender. Transfer to a warmed serving dish and keep hot.

Add the lemon juice and stock to the pan juices, bring to the boil, stirring, and boil for 1 minute. Add the parsley and remaining butter and stir until blended.

Pour over the chicken and garnish with lemon slices to serve.

Serves 4

Chicken with Rosemary; Chicken Breasts with Lemon

Green Pepper Steak

CHICKEN LIVER PILAFF

25 g (1 oz) butter
125 g (4 oz) streaky bacon, derinded and chopped
2 cloves garlic, thinly sliced
250 g (8 oz) chicken livers, chopped
50 g (2 oz) button mushrooms, sliced
250 ml (8 fl oz) dry white wine
bouquet garni
175 g (6 oz) long-grain rice
salt and pepper
300 ml (½ pint) chicken stock
3 tablespoons single cream
2 tablespoons chopped parsley

Melt the butter in a pan, add the bacon and sauté gently for 2 minutes. Add the garlic and chicken livers and cook for 5 minutes, stirring occasionally. Add the mushrooms, wine, bouquet garni, rice and salt and pepper to taste. Stir in the stock, bring to the boil, cover and simmer for 12 minutes.

Remove the lid, increase the heat, and stir until the rice is just tender and all the liquid has been absorbed. Discard the bouquet garni.

Just before serving, stir in the cream and parsley and serve immediately.

Serves 4 to 6

GREEN PEPPER STEAK

2 × 150 g (5 oz) sirloin or fillet steaks
salt
2 tablespoons green peppercorns
1 tablespoon chopped thyme
1 clove garlic, crushed
50 g (2 oz) button mushrooms, sliced
120 ml (4 fl oz) dry red wine
dash of Worcestershire sauce
1 teaspoon French mustard
2 spring onions, chopped
thyme sprigs to garnish

Season the steaks with salt. Press in the peppercorns and thyme.

Cook under a preheated hot grill for 2 to 3 minutes on each side, until browned, or until cooked according to taste.

Meanwhile, put the garlic, mushrooms and wine in a pan and bring to the boil. Boil rapidly until reduced and thickened, then stir in the Worcestershire sauce, mustard and spring onions.

Arrange the steaks on a warmed serving dish and spoon over the sauce. Garnish with thyme and serve immediately, with a green salad or vegetable.

Serves 2

FRANKFURTER AND BEAN HOT POT

25 g (1 oz) butter
1 large onion, chopped
2 bacon rashers, derinded and chopped
4 frankfurters, diced
125 g (4 oz) garlic sausage, diced
1 tablespoon capers, chopped
2 × 439 g (15½ oz) cans red kidney beans, drained
150 ml (¼ pint) light stock
salt and pepper
2 tablespoons chopped fresh parsley

Melt the butter in a flameproof casserole, add the onion and bacon and fry gently until soft. Add the frankfurters, garlic sausage, capers and kidney beans. Mix well.

Stir in the stock. Cover and cook in a preheated moderate oven, 180°C (350°F), Gas Mark 4, for 20 minutes.

Check the seasoning and stir in the parsley. Serve immediately, accompanied by crusty French bread.

Serves 4

CHICKEN WITH WALNUTS

2 tablespoons oil
2 cloves garlic, sliced
1 small piece root ginger, shredded
4 spring onions, roughly chopped
4 large boneless chicken breasts, thinly sliced
50 g (2 oz) shelled walnuts, roughly chopped
1 small red pepper, cored, seeded, and thinly sliced
2 courgettes, thinly sliced
50 g (2 oz) button mushrooms
50 g (2 oz) mangetout
2 tablespoons soy sauce
1 tablespoon dry sherry

Heat the oil in a large frying pan or wok, add the garlic, ginger and spring onions and fry for 1 minute. Add the chicken and cook for 5 minutes, until browned on all sides. Add the remaining ingredients, increase the heat and cook, stirring constantly, for 3 minutes.

Turn into a warmed serving dish and serve immediately, with noodles or rice.

Serves 4

FILLET STEAKS WITH STILTON

75 g (3 oz) blue Stilton cheese
75 g (3 oz) butter, softened
1 tablespoon port
1 teaspoon chopped chives
1 teaspoon chopped thyme
½ clove garlic, crushed
salt and pepper
6 × 2.5 cm (1 inch) fillet steaks
thyme sprigs to garnish

Put the cheese, butter and port into a blender or food processor and blend until smooth. Stir in the herbs, garlic and salt and pepper to taste. Form the mixture into a roll, wrap in foil and chill in the ice compartment of the refrigerator for 20 minutes.

Season the steaks with salt and pepper and cook under a preheated hot grill for 3 to 5 minutes on each side, according to taste. Arrange on a warmed serving dish.

Cut the herb butter into 6 and place on the steaks. Garnish with thyme and serve immediately, with courgettes.

Serves 6

Lamb Cutlets with Sherry Sauce

LAMB CUTLETS WITH SHERRY SAUCE

8 lamb cutlets
1 clove garlic, sliced
1 egg, beaten
50 g (2 oz) dry white breadcrumbs
1–2 tablespoons oil
25 g (1 oz) unsalted butter
1 tablespoon chopped thyme
1 tablespoon chopped parsley
1 tablespoon chopped sage
1 tablespoon chopped chives
150 ml (¼ pint) dry sherry
1 × 142 ml (5 fl oz) double cream
salt and pepper
TO GARNISH:
125 g (4 oz) green olives
sage leaves

Cut small slits in the cutlets and push in the garlic. Coat each cutlet with egg and breadcrumbs, then chill for 20 minutes.

Heat the oil and butter in a frying pan, add the cutlets and brown on both sides. Lower the heat and cook for 6 minutes on each side. Drain on kitchen paper and arrange on a warmed serving dish; keep warm.

Add the herbs and sherry to the pan and boil rapidly for 2 minutes, until thickened. Stir in the cream, and salt and pepper to taste.

Spoon over the cutlets and serve immediately, garnished with the olives and sage.

Serves 4

PORK CHOPS WITH MUSTARD SAUCE

25 g (1 oz) butter
1 onion, finely sliced
plain flour for coating
salt and pepper
4 pork chops
120 ml (4 fl oz) medium sherry
175 ml (6 fl oz) chicken stock
2 tablespoons mild French mustard

Melt the butter in a flameproof casserole, add the onion and fry until soft. Remove with a slotted spoon and set aside.

Season the flour with salt and pepper and use to coat the chops. Add to the casserole and fry briskly until browned on both sides.

Return the onion to the casserole and add the sherry and stock. Cover and simmer for 30 minutes, or until the chops are cooked.

Transfer the chops to a warmed serving dish, using a slotted spoon. Add the mustard to the sauce in the casserole, stir well and check the seasoning. Pour over the chops and serve immediately.

Serves 4

PORK FILLET WITH PLUMS

plain flour for coating
salt and pepper
500 g (1 lb) pork fillet, cut into 4 pieces
50 g (2 oz) butter
1 × 567 g (20 oz) can Victoria plums, drained and stoned
$\frac{1}{4}$ teaspoon ground cinnamon
150 ml ($\frac{1}{4}$ pint) red wine
chopped parsley to garnish

Season the flour with salt and pepper and use to coat the pork.

Melt the butter in a frying pan, add the pork and fry until golden brown on both sides. Transfer to a casserole.

Mash the plums to a coarse purée. Stir in the cinnamon and wine and pour over the pork. Cover and cook in a preheated moderate oven, 180°C (350°F), Gas Mark 4, for 30 minutes.

Serve hot, garnished with parsley.

Serves 4

Pork Chops with Mustard Sauce; Pork Fillet with Plums

VEAL STROGANOFF

4 veal escalopes
50 g (2 oz) butter
1 onion, sliced
125 g (4 oz) button mushrooms, sliced
1–2 tablespoons tomato purée
1 tablespoon plain flour
1 × 142 ml (5 fl oz) carton fresh soured cream
salt and pepper
1–2 tablespoons lemon juice
watercress sprigs to garnish

Beat the escalopes until thin, then cut into short strips.

Melt half the butter in a frying pan, add the onion and mushrooms and fry until soft. Stir in the tomato purée and flour. Cook, stirring, over low heat for 2 to 3 minutes. Remove from the heat.

Melt the remaining butter in a clean pan, add the veal and fry over high heat, turning, until evenly browned. Add the meat to the sauce and stir well. Add the cream, salt, pepper and lemon juice to taste.

Garnish with watercress. Serve immediately, with buttered noodles or plain boiled rice.

Serves 4

BARBECUED LAMB CUTLETS

4 drops Tabasco sauce
2 teaspoons chilli powder
2 teaspoons salt
1½ tablespoons soft brown sugar
1½ tablespoons Worcestershire sauce
2 tablespoons tomato ketchup
1½ tablespoons wine vinegar
4 tablespoons water
8 lamb cutlets, trimmed

Mix the Tabasco, chilli powder, salt and brown sugar together in a large dish. Gradually stir in the Worcestershire sauce, tomato ketchup, vinegar and water. Add the cutlets and turn to coat thoroughly. Leave to marinate for 4 hours.

Transfer the cutlets to a grill rack and brush with the marinade. Cook under a preheated hot grill for 5 to 10 minutes on each side, depending on the thickness of the cutlets, basting frequently with the marinade.

Serve immediately with plain boiled rice or buttered noodles.

Serves 4

Tyrolean Veal with Soured Cream

TYROLEAN VEAL WITH SOURED CREAM

2 tablespoons plain flour
salt and pepper
4 veal escalopes
50 g (2 oz) butter
1 small onion, finely chopped
2 tablespoons capers, with their vinegar
200 ml (⅓ pint) water
5 tablespoons fresh soured cream
chopped parsley to garnish

Season half the flour with salt and pepper and use to coat the escalopes.

Melt half the butter in a frying pan, add the veal and fry gently for about 5 minutes on each side until tender and golden. Remove and set aside.

Melt the remaining butter in the pan, add the onion and fry until soft. Add the remaining flour and cook, stirring, for 1 to 2 minutes.

Add the capers in their vinegar and the water and cook until the sauce thickens. Stir in the soured cream. Return the veal to the pan and heat through gently.

Sprinkle with parsley and serve with plain boiled rice.

Serves 4

Chicken and Walnut Salad

CHICKEN AND WALNUT SALAD

500 g (1 lb) cooked boned chicken, cut into pieces
2 celery sticks, coarsely chopped
1 large dessert apple, cored and diced
50 g (2 oz) shelled walnuts, roughly chopped
6 tablespoons Mayonnaise (see page 21)
1–2 tablespoons single cream
watercress sprigs to garnish

Put the chicken pieces into a large bowl with the celery, apple and walnuts.

Thin the Mayonnaise to give the consistency of thick cream, by adding a little single cream. Pour over the chicken and toss well until the ingredients are evenly coated.

Turn into a serving dish and garnish with watercress.

Serves 4

CHICKEN WITH ORANGES AND ALMONDS

50 g (2 oz) butter
50 g (2 oz) flaked almonds
4 chicken portions
salt and pepper
paprika
3 oranges
2 teaspoons caster sugar

Melt the butter in a pan, add the almonds and fry gently until golden. Remove the almonds and set aside.

Sprinkle the chicken with salt, pepper and paprika to taste. Add to the fat remaining in the pan and fry, turning, until golden all over. Cover and cook gently for 30 minutes, or until tender.

Meanwhile, squeeze the juice from 2 of the oranges. Carefully cut the third orange into segments.

Transfer the chicken to a warmed serving dish and keep hot.

Add the orange juice, orange segments and sugar to the pan juices and boil rapidly for 2 minutes. Pour over the chicken. Sprinkle with the almonds and serve immediately.

Serves 4

SPICED COUNTRY CHICKEN

4 chicken portions
plain flour for coating
25 g (1 oz) butter
1 onion, finely chopped
1 clove garlic, crushed
1 green pepper, cored, seeded and chopped
2 teaspoons curry powder
1 teaspoon chopped thyme
1 × 227 g (8 oz) can tomatoes
2 tablespoons sweet white vermouth
salt and pepper
50 g (2 oz) raisins

Coat the chicken portions with flour. Melt the butter in a large pan, add the chicken and fry briskly until golden all over. Remove from the pan and set aside.

Add the onion, garlic, green pepper, curry powder and thyme to the fat remaining in the pan and fry, stirring, for 5 minutes.

Add the tomatoes with their juice and the vermouth. Return the chicken to the pan and add salt and pepper to taste. Cover and cook for 20 minutes, or until the chicken is tender.

Stir in the raisins and serve hot, with jacket potatoes or plain boiled rice.

Serves 4

CHILLI CHICKEN LIVERS

1 tablespoon oil
1 large onion
2 cloves garlic, crushed
1 × 397 g (14 oz) can tomatoes
1 tablespoon tomato purée
1 teaspoon dried mixed herbs
1–2 teaspoons chilli powder
1 chilli, seeded and roughly chopped
salt and pepper
350 g (12 oz) chicken livers
plain flour for coating
25 g (1 oz) butter
125 g (4 oz) button mushrooms, sliced
150 ml (¼ pint) dry white wine

Heat the oil in a pan. Slice the onion thinly and add it to the pan with the garlic and cook for 5 minutes, until transparent but not browned. Stir in the tomatoes with their juice. Bring to the boil and cook rapidly for 5 minutes. Stir in the tomato purée, herbs, chilli powder, chilli, and salt and pepper to taste. Bring back to the boil and cook, uncovered, for 20 minutes.

Roughly chop the chicken livers and coat with the flour. Melt the butter in a pan, add the chicken livers and fry for 5 minutes, until lightly browned. Drain them on kitchen paper, then add to the tomato sauce with the mushrooms and wine. Bring to the boil and boil rapidly for 5 to 7 minutes.

Check the seasoning and serve with noodles or rice.

Serves 4 to 6

CHILLI CON CARNE

50 g (2 oz) butter
2 large onions, finely chopped
2 cloves garlic, crushed
500 g (1 lb) minced beef
2 teaspoons chilli powder
4 teaspoons cumin powder
1 × 64 g (2¼ oz) can tomato purée
2 × 439 g (15½ oz) cans red kidney beans, drained
300 ml (½ pint) beef stock
salt and pepper
chopped parsley to garnish

Melt the butter in a flameproof casserole. Add the onions and garlic and fry gently for 5 minutes until golden. Stir in the beef and cook, stirring, for 10 minutes.

Mix together the chilli powder, cumin and tomato purée and stir into the beef. Add the kidney beans, stock and salt and pepper to taste.

Cover and cook in a preheated moderate oven, 180°C (350°F), Gas Mark 4, for 25 minutes.

Sprinkle with chopped parsley and serve hot with plain boiled rice or crusty French bread.

Serves 4

Liver and Bacon with Apple Rings

LIVER AND BACON WITH APPLE RINGS

50 g (2 oz) butter
2 large cooking apples, peeled, cored and cut into thick rings
500 g (1 lb) calves' liver, sliced
4 rashers lean bacon, derinded

Melt half the butter in a frying pan, add the apple rings and fry gently until soft. Transfer to a warmed dish; keep hot.

Melt the remaining butter in the pan, add the liver and fry gently for about 2 minutes on each side until tender.

Meanwhile, cook the bacon under a preheated medium grill until crisp.

Transfer the liver to a warmed serving dish. Arrange the apple rings on top and the bacon around the edge. Serve immediately.

Serves 4

STEAK WITH VEGETABLES

4 × 175 g (6 oz) grilling steaks
1½–2 tablespoons oil
1 onion, thinly sliced
1 carrot, thinly sliced
2 potatoes, thinly sliced
4 tablespoons hot water (approximately)
2 celery sticks, sliced
4–6 spring cabbage or spinach leaves, shredded
50 g (2 oz) small broccoli or cauliflower florets
50 g (2 oz) mushrooms, sliced
¼ cucumber, sliced
2–3 tomatoes, cut into wedges
1½–2 tablespoons soy sauce

Cook the steak under a preheated hot grill for 3 to 5 minutes on each side, depending on thickness and personal taste.

Heat the oil in a large frying pan, add the onion and fry for 2 minutes. Add the carrot, potatoes and about 4 tablespoons hot water and stir-fry over a high heat for 3 minutes, turning the vegetables using two large wooden spoons. Add the celery, cabbage or spinach, and broccoli or cauliflower, and stir-fry for 2 minutes, adding a little more water if necessary to prevent sticking. Add the mushrooms, cucumber and tomatoes and stir-fry for another minute. Add the soy sauce and stir well.

The vegetables should be tender but still crisp, with a rich gravy in the bottom of the pan. Serve hot with the steak on warmed plates.

Serves 4

BEEF WITH PLUMS

1 tablespoon oil
1 onion, thinly sliced
1 clove garlic, crushed
2–3 pieces beef for beef olives, cut into thin slivers
2–3 dessert plums, stoned and cut into slices
2 or 3 mushrooms, thinly sliced
1 tablespoon sherry
2 teaspoons soft brown sugar
1 tablespoon soy sauce
2 teaspoons cornflour
2 tablespoons water
chopped spring onion tops to garnish

Heat the oil in a large frying pan, add the onion and fry for 2 minutes. Stir in the garlic, then push the mixture to one side of the pan. Tilt the pan to let the juices run out of the onion and over the base. Scatter in the meat strips and stir-fry over a high heat for 2 minutes, until the meat is evenly coloured.

Lower the heat and add the plums and mushrooms. Continue to stir-fry for 1 minute, then stir in the sherry, sugar and soy sauce. Blend the cornflour with the water and add to the pan. Cook, stirring, until the sauce has thickened.

Garnish with spring onions and serve with wholewheat tagliatelle and green vegetables such as broccoli, spinach and French beans.

Serves 4

BELOW: *Steak with Vegetables; Beef with Plums*
RIGHT: *Veal in Red Gravy; Beef and Orange Kebabs*

VEAL IN RED GRAVY

1 tablespoon oil
1 small onion, finely chopped
1 clove garlic, crushed
2.5 cm (1 inch) piece root ginger, peeled and chopped very finely, or ½ teaspoon dried ginger
3 veal escalopes, cut into matchstick pieces
1 heaped tablespoon tomato purée
1 tablespoon soy sauce
pepper
1 tablespoon sweet sherry
3 tablespoons water
1 teaspoon sugar (optional)
spring onion strips to garnish

Heat the oil in a large frying pan, add the onion and fry gently for about 30 seconds. Add the garlic and ginger and stir-fry for 30 seconds. Push the mixture to one side of the pan and tilt the pan to let the juices run out over the base.

Scatter in the veal strips and increase the heat. Cook, stirring, for about 2 minutes, until the veal is evenly coloured.

Lower the heat and stir in the remaining ingredients, adding sugar, if wished. Cook, stirring, for 30 seconds. Garnish with spring onion strips and serve immediately.

Serves 4

BEEF AND ORANGE KEBABS

500 g (1 lb) frying steak, cut into bite-sized pieces
2–3 tomatoes, quartered
½ green pepper, cored, seeded and cut into pieces
½ red pepper, cored, seeded and cut into pieces
125 g (4 oz) button mushrooms
1 onion, cut into segments
2 tablespoons oil
grated rind and juice of 1 orange
1 tablespoon soft brown sugar
1 tablespoon soy sauce
pepper
watercress to garnish

Thread the meat and vegetables alternately on 4 to 6 long skewers or 8 to 12 average size, starting with tomato.

Mix together the oil, orange rind and juice, sugar, soy sauce and pepper and use to coat the kebabs, brushing on with a pastry brush. Cook under a preheated moderate grill, about 7.5 cm (3 inches) away from the heat, for about 15 minutes; brush the kebabs with the oil and orange mixture after 10 minutes and turn over. Garnish with watercress.

Serve with crusty French bread and a green salad.

Serves 4 to 6

LEAFY SALADS

Fresh simple salads make a good alternative to cooked vegetables to serve with main course dishes and there is an increasingly wide range to be found in the shops these days. Use fresh leaves, such as frisé, cos or iceberg lettuce, rocket, radicchio, watercress and chicory, singly or in combination. Rinse the leaves, pat them dry with a towel and tear large leaves into small pieces. Tumble into a bowl and combine with French Dressing (see page 15) or Vinaigrette Dressing (see page 37). Dress the leaves just before serving and toss thoroughly to coat each one with the chosen dressing.

CRISP-TOPPED MUSHROOMS

2 tablespoons oil
500 g (1 lb) small mushrooms
1 onion, finely chopped
2 small cloves garlic, crushed
3 slices wholewheat bread, crusts removed, made into crumbs
2 slices lean ham, cut into small squares
1 heaped tablespoon chopped parsley
pepper
about 2 tablespoons grated Parmesan cheese
TO GARNISH:
watercress sprigs
mushroom slices

Heat half the oil in a pan, add the mushrooms and fry gently for 4 to 5 minutes. Place in a flameproof dish and keep warm.

Heat the remaining oil in the pan, add the onion and stir-fry for 2 to 3 minutes. Stir in the garlic, breadcrumbs, ham, parsley and pepper to taste. Mix well and spoon over the mushrooms.

Sprinkle with the Parmesan cheese and place under a preheated hot grill until the cheese has melted and the topping is crisp. Garnish with the watercress and mushrooms and serve with a green salad.

Serves 4

STIR-FRIED LAMB WITH ROSEMARY

2 teaspoons oil
1 onion, finely chopped
2 cloves garlic, crushed
2–3 large lamb chump chops, cut into small cubes
2 teaspoons soy sauce
1 rosemary sprig, finely chopped, or 1 teaspoon dried rosemary
2 teaspoons cornflour
3 tablespoons water
150 ml ($\frac{1}{4}$ pint) hot water
rosemary sprig to garnish

Heat the oil in a pan, add the onion and stir-fry for 2 minutes. Stir in the garlic. Push the mixture to one side of the pan and scatter in the meat cubes. Stir-fry for about 3 to 4 minutes, until evenly browned. Push to one side and tilt the pan so the fat runs out of the meat. Mop up this excess fat with kitchen paper while the pan is off the heat.

Mix the meat with the onions and move back into the centre of the pan. Add the soy sauce and the rosemary and stir-fry for a few seconds. Transfer to warmed serving plates using a slotted spoon and keep warm.

Blend the cornflour with the water and pour into the pan. Stir to release any pan juices. Add the hot water and simmer, stirring, until thickened.

Spoon over the meat and garnish with rosemary.

Serves 4

LEFT: *Stir-Fried Lamb with Rosemary; Crisp-Topped Mushrooms*
RIGHT: *Duck with Passion Fruit; Chicken with Lemon*

DUCK WITH PASSION FRUIT

1 tablespoon oil
1 onion, thinly sliced
1 clove garlic, crushed
2 duck breasts, skinned and cut into thin slivers
1 passion fruit, halved and sieved
juice of 1 orange
2 teaspoons sugar
1 tablespoon soy sauce
pepper
2 teaspoons cornflour
5 tablespoons water
orange twists or nasturtium flowers to garnish

Heat the oil in a pan, add the onion and cook, stirring, for 2 minutes. Stir in the garlic, then push to one side of the pan. Tilt the pan to let the juices run out and over the base.

Increase the heat, add the slivers of duck to the pan and stir-fry for 3 minutes, until they have lost their pink colour. Lower the heat and add the passion fruit, orange juice, sugar, soy sauce and pepper to taste. Blend the cornflour with the water and add to the pan. Stir until thickened.

Garnish each portion with a twist of orange, or a nasturtium flower if available.

Serves 4

CHICKEN WITH LEMON

1 tablespoon oil
1 onion, finely chopped
1 clove garlic, crushed
2–3 chicken breasts, skinned and cut into thin slices
1 tablespoon soy sauce
50 g (2 oz) small button mushrooms, sliced
finely grated rind of 1 lemon
4 tablespoons water
2 tablespoons single cream or milk
pepper
watercress sprigs to garnish

Heat the oil in a pan, add the onion and cook, stirring, for 2 minutes. Stir in the garlic and push to one side of the pan. Tilt the pan to let the juices run out over the base.

Add the chicken and stir-fry for 2 minutes over a high heat. Lower the heat, add the soy sauce and mushrooms and stir-fry for 1 minute. Stir in the lemon rind and water, then add the cream or milk and heat through gently, without boiling. Add pepper to taste. Garnish with watercress and serve immediately.

Serves 4

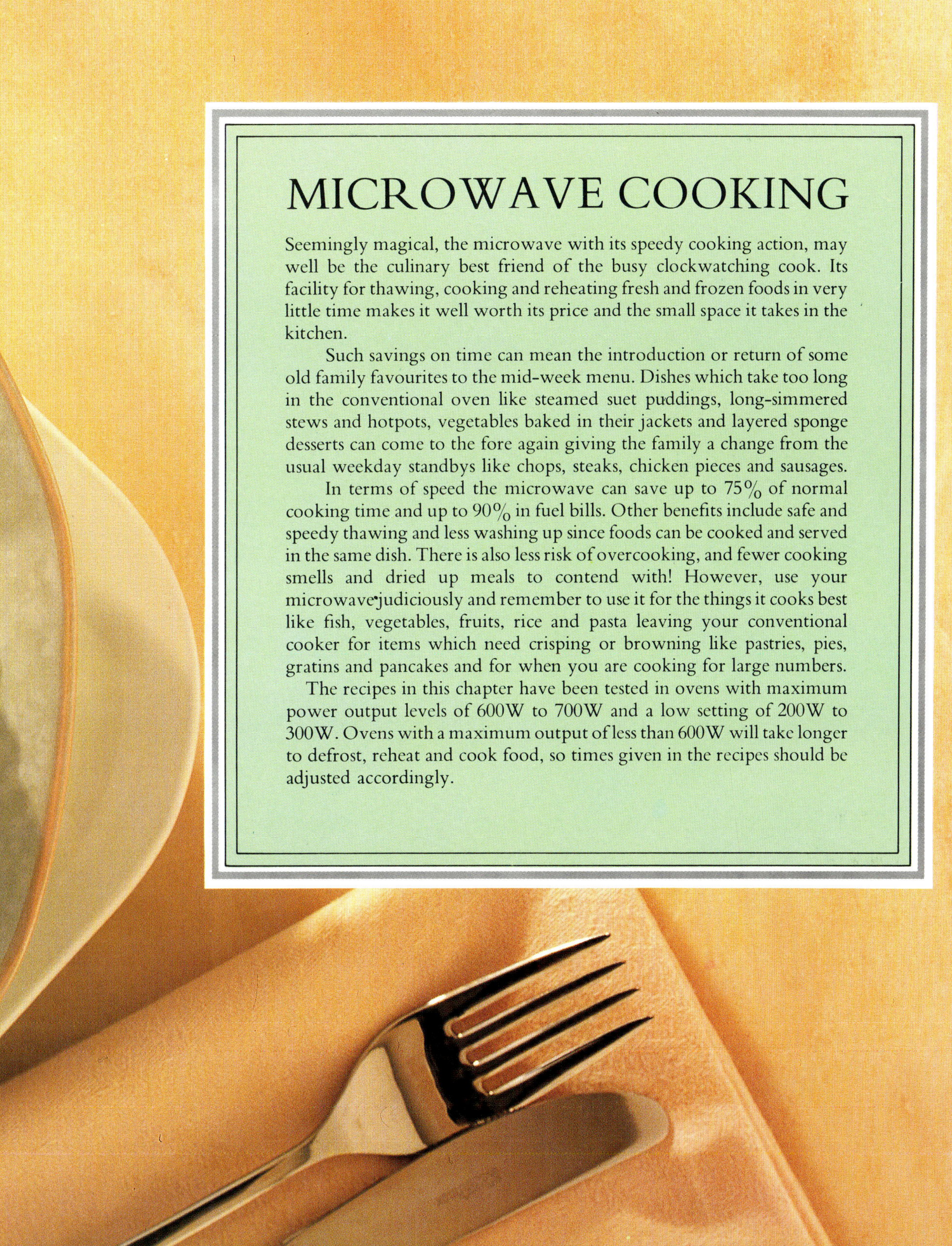

MICROWAVE COOKING

Seemingly magical, the microwave with its speedy cooking action, may well be the culinary best friend of the busy clockwatching cook. Its facility for thawing, cooking and reheating fresh and frozen foods in very little time makes it well worth its price and the small space it takes in the kitchen.

Such savings on time can mean the introduction or return of some old family favourites to the mid-week menu. Dishes which take too long in the conventional oven like steamed suet puddings, long-simmered stews and hotpots, vegetables baked in their jackets and layered sponge desserts can come to the fore again giving the family a change from the usual weekday standbys like chops, steaks, chicken pieces and sausages.

In terms of speed the microwave can save up to 75% of normal cooking time and up to 90% in fuel bills. Other benefits include safe and speedy thawing and less washing up since foods can be cooked and served in the same dish. There is also less risk of overcooking, and fewer cooking smells and dried up meals to contend with! However, use your microwave judiciously and remember to use it for the things it cooks best like fish, vegetables, fruits, rice and pasta leaving your conventional cooker for items which need crisping or browning like pastries, pies, gratins and pancakes and for when you are cooking for large numbers.

The recipes in this chapter have been tested in ovens with maximum power output levels of 600W to 700W and a low setting of 200W to 300W. Ovens with a maximum output of less than 600W will take longer to defrost, reheat and cook food, so times given in the recipes should be adjusted accordingly.

POTATO AND WATERCRESS SOUP

25 g (1 oz) butter
1 onion, finely chopped
1 bunch of watercress, finely chopped
500 g (1 lb) potatoes, diced
600 ml (1 pint) chicken stock
salt and pepper
120 ml (4 fl oz) single cream

Melt the butter in a large casserole on HIGH for 30 seconds. Add the onion, cover and cook on HIGH for $1\frac{1}{2}$ minutes.

Add the watercress, potatoes, stock, and salt and pepper to taste. Cover and cook on HIGH for about 15 minutes or until the vegetables are cooked.

Sieve or work in an electric blender or food processor until smooth. Return to the casserole.

Stir in the cream and cook on LOW for 3 to 4 minutes or until heated through; do not allow to boil.

Pour into a tureen. Serve hot or cold, with garlic bread.

Serves 4

POTATO AND ROQUEFORT SALAD

500 g (1 lb) new potatoes
2 tablespoons water
350 g (12 oz) tomatoes, chopped
6 spring onions, chopped
3 tablespoons Roquefort Dressing (see right)
spring onions to garnish

Prick the potato skins with a fork. Put into a casserole dish with the water, cover and cook on HIGH for 10 to 12 minutes, until tender. Drain, cut into large pieces while still warm and place in a salad bowl.

Add the tomatoes, spring onions and Roquefort Dressing and toss well. Chill until required. Serve, garnished with spring onions, as a starter or accompaniment.

Serves 4 to 6

LEFT: *Potato and Watercress Soup; Potato and Roquefort Salad*
RIGHT: *Cod Steaks Niçoise*

FRENCH ONION SOUP

500 g (1 lb) onions, thinly sliced
50 g (2 oz) butter
salt and pepper
150 ml ($\frac{1}{4}$ pint) white wine
600 ml (1 pint) boiling beef stock
$\frac{1}{4}$ teaspoon dried oregano
6 slices French bread, toasted and buttered
125 g (4 oz) Cheddar cheese, grated
chilli powder (optional)

Put the onions, butter and salt and pepper to taste into a large bowl, cover and cook on HIGH for 6 to 7 minutes. Divide the onions between 6 soup bowls.

Mix the wine and stock together, add the oregano and pour over the onions. Cover the bowls and cook on HIGH for 10 to 12 minutes.

Place a slice of toast in each bowl, buttered side up, and sprinkle with cheese. Either place under a conventional grill until golden, or place in the microwave oven for 2 to 3 minutes, until melted.

Sprinkle with chilli powder, if liked, to serve.

Serves 6

ROQUEFORT DRESSING

50 g (2 oz) Roquefort cheese
1 × 142 ml (5 fl oz) single cream
1 tablespoon chopped chives
salt and pepper

Mash the cheese with a fork and gradually add the cream to form a smooth paste. Mix in the chives and salt and pepper to taste.

Makes 250 ml (8 fl oz)

MICROWAVE SHORT CUTS FOR SAVOURY DISHES

The microwave is an invaluable aid for making short cuts.

To brown nuts quickly for garnishes without heating the grill, place 50 g (2 oz) whole or flaked nuts on a flat dish and cook the whole nuts on HIGH for 5–6 minutes and the flaked nuts for 3–5 minutes.

A semi-soft cheese like a Camembert or a Brie can be instantly ripened for cooking or for serving on a cheeseboard. Depending on its state of ripeness, cook a 250 g (8 oz) quantity on LOW for 15–45 seconds.

Butter and margarine can be softened for easy creaming or spreading; simply cook a 125 g (4 oz) quantity on HIGH for 15–30 seconds.

COD STEAKS NIÇOISE

1 tablespoon vegetable oil
1 onion, chopped
1 clove garlic, crushed
1 tablespoon chopped parsley
1 × 227 g (8 oz) can tomatoes, drained and chopped
150 ml ($\frac{1}{4}$ pint) dry white wine
salt and pepper
2 × 250 g (8 oz) cod steaks
TO GARNISH:
2 black olives
parsley sprigs

Put the oil, onion and garlic into a bowl. Cover and cook on HIGH for $1\frac{1}{2}$ minutes. Stir in the parsley, tomatoes, wine, and salt and pepper to taste. Cover and cook on HIGH for 2 minutes.

Arrange the cod steaks in a serving dish and pour over the sauce. Cover and cook on HIGH for 6 minutes. Leave to stand for 2 to 3 minutes.

Place a black olive in the centre of each steak and garnish with parsley sprigs. Serve with boiled new potatoes and broccoli.

Serves 2

NOTE: Fish is particularly good cooked in the microwave oven, because its texture and flavour are well retained.

SARDINE AND TOMATO QUICHE

1 × 18 cm (7 inch) pre-baked pastry case
2 tomatoes, sliced
2 × 120 g (4 oz) cans sardines in oil, drained
1 egg
150 ml ($\frac{1}{4}$ pint) warmed milk
salt and pepper
TO GARNISH:
tomato slices
watercress sprigs

Place the pastry case on a flat plate and cover the base with the tomato slices. Arrange the sardines on top.
Beat the egg in a small bowl, stir in the milk, and season with salt and pepper to taste. Pour over the fish.

Cook on LOW for 12 to 15 minutes or until the centre is just set; rotate the dish during cooking if the oven does not have a turntable. Leave to stand for 5 minutes.

Garnish with tomato slices and watercress sprigs. Serve hot or cold with salad.

Serves 4

SMOKED HADDOCK WITH PRAWN SAUCE

2 × 150 g (6 oz) packs frozen smoked haddock
25 g (1 oz) butter
25 g (1 oz) plain flour
300 ml ($\frac{1}{2}$ pint) milk
salt and pepper
125 g (4 oz) peeled prawns

Cut a small slit in the bags of smoked haddock and place on a plate. Cook on HIGH for 9 to 10 minutes or until the fish is cooked; rotate the plate after 5 minutes if the oven does not have a turntable. Leave the fish to stand in the bags while making the sauce.

Put the butter into a jug in the oven on HIGH for 1 to 1$\frac{1}{2}$ minutes until melted. Blend in the flour and gradually stir in the milk. Season with salt and pepper to taste and cook on HIGH for 2 minutes, stirring after 1 minute. Stir in the prawns and cook on HIGH for 3 to 4 minutes, stirring every minute.

Place the fish on individual warmed serving plates and pour over the prawn sauce. Serve with green beans and croquette potatoes.

Serves 2

Sardine and Tomato Quiche; Smoked Haddock with Prawn Sauce

STUFFED RAINBOW TROUT

4 rainbow trout, thawed if frozen
garlic salt
1 green pepper, cored, seeded and sliced
1 onion, sliced
2 tomatoes, sliced
75 g (3 oz) peeled prawns
TO GARNISH:
25 g (1 oz) flaked almonds, toasted
watercress sprigs
lemon wedges

Wipe the trout inside and outside with kitchen paper. Sprinkle the cavities with garlic salt. Mix together the green pepper, onion, tomatoes and prawns and use to stuff the trout.

Cover the tails with small pieces of foil and arrange the fish in a dish in a single layer. Place small circles of foil over the eyes to prevent them 'popping' during cooking. Score the skin to prevent bursting.

Cover and cook on HIGH for 10 to 12 minutes or until the flesh can be easily separated with a fork; rearrange halfway through cooking if the oven does not have a turntable. Leave to stand for 2 to 3 minutes.

Garnish with the toasted flaked almonds, watercress and lemon wedges and serve with salad.

Serves 4

TUNA AND MUSHROOM PIE

25 g (1 oz) butter
125 g (4 oz) mushrooms, sliced
1 × 298 g ($10\frac{1}{2}$ oz) can condensed cream of mushroom soup
2 tablespoons single cream
2 × 198 g (7 oz) cans tuna steak, drained and flaked
3 teaspoons lemon juice
salt and pepper
500 g (1 lb) potatoes, cooked and mashed

Melt the butter in a casserole on HIGH for about 30 seconds. Stir in the mushrooms, cover and cook on HIGH for 1 to $1\frac{1}{2}$ minutes, until soft. Stir in the remaining ingredients, except the mashed potato, seasoning with salt and pepper to taste.

Cover and cook on HIGH for 3 to 4 minutes or until hot, stirring after $1\frac{1}{2}$ minutes.

Level the mixture in the dish and pipe or spread the hot mashed potato on top. If liked, place under a preheated conventional grill to brown. Serve with green beans.

Serves 4

Fish Fillets with Almonds

FISH FILLETS WITH ALMONDS

50 g (2 oz) butter
25 g (1 oz) flaked almonds
500 g (1 lb) white fish fillets
pinch of dried thyme
pinch of onion salt
2 teaspoons lemon juice
thyme sprigs

Put the butter and almonds into a dish and cook on HIGH for about 5 minutes or until the almonds are golden, stirring occasionally. Remove with a slotted spoon and set aside.

Arrange the fish in the dish with the thickest parts towards the outside. Turn to coat in the butter. Add the thyme, onion salt and lemon juice.

Cover and cook on HIGH for 5 to 6 minutes or until the fish flakes easily.

Sprinkle with the almonds and garnish with thyme sprigs. Serve with piped creamed potatoes and courgettes or peas.

Serves 4

Lamb in Onion Sauce

LAMB IN ONION SAUCE

50 g (2 oz) butter
1 onion, sliced
625 g ($1\frac{1}{4}$ lb) boned lean leg of lamb, cubed
2 tablespoons plain flour
1 teaspoon wine vinegar
300 ml ($\frac{1}{2}$ pint) boiling chicken stock
1 tablespoon chopped rosemary
salt and pepper
rosemary sprigs to garnish

Melt the butter in a casserole on HIGH for 1 minute. Stir in the onion and cook on HIGH for 2 minutes. Stir in the lamb and cook on HIGH for 7 minutes, stirring twice.

Stir in the flour and vinegar, mixing well. Carefully stir in the chicken stock, rosemary, and salt and pepper to taste.

Cover and cook on HIGH for 10 minutes or until the lamb is cooked and the sauce has thickened, stirring occasionally. Leave to stand, covered, for 5 minutes.

Check the seasoning and garnish with rosemary sprigs. Serve with green ribbon noodles or boiled rice.

Serves 4

LIVER, BACON AND ONIONS

4 rashers back bacon, derinded and cut into 5 cm (2 inch) pieces
50 g (2 oz) plain flour
salt and pepper
500 g (1 lb) lambs' liver, sliced
2 onions, sliced
120 ml (4 fl oz) water
1 teaspoon dried mixed herbs
2 tablespoons tomato purée

Put the bacon into a dish, cover loosely with kitchen paper and cook on HIGH for 4 minutes.

Season the flour with salt and pepper and use to coat the liver.

Drain all but 2 tablespoons bacon fat from the dish and put the liver into the dish. Add the remaining ingredients. Cover and cook on HIGH for 5 minutes, stir and continue cooking for 5 to 7 minutes, until the liver is cooked. Leave to stand, covered, for 5 minutes.

Serve with creamed potatoes or boiled rice, and peas or mangetout.

Serves 4

TURKEY TETRAZZINI

4 rashers streaky bacon, derinded
4 tablespoons oil
125 g (4 oz) mushrooms, sliced
1 onion, chopped
4 tablespoons plain flour
salt and pepper
350 ml (12 fl oz) boiling chicken stock
350 ml (12 fl oz) milk
3 tablespoons dry sherry
250 g (8 oz) spaghetti, cooked and drained
350 g (12 oz) cooked turkey, cubed
50 g (2 oz) grated Parmesan cheese

Snip the bacon fat at regular intervals and place the rashers between a double thickness of kitchen paper on a plate. Cook on HIGH for 4 to 5 minutes or until crisp. Crumble and set aside.

Put the oil into a large casserole, add the mushrooms and onion and cook on HIGH for 4 minutes or until the onion is tender, stirring once.

Stir in the flour, and salt and pepper to taste and cook on HIGH for 30 seconds. Add the stock and milk, mix well and cook on HIGH until bubbling and thickened, stirring during cooking.

Stir in the sherry, spaghetti, turkey, bacon and cheese, mixing well. Cover and cook on HIGH for 10 to 12 minutes or until heated through, stirring once.

Serves 4

CHICKEN PAPRIKA

1 × 1–1.5 kg (2–3½ lb) chicken, jointed
2 tablespoons oil
1 large onion, chopped
1 green pepper, cored, seeded and chopped
1 tablespoon mild paprika
1 tablespoon tomato purée
2 large tomatoes, skinned and chopped
150 ml (¼ pint) chicken stock
salt and pepper
2 tablespoons natural low-fat yogurt
parsley sprig to garnish

Arrange the chicken joints in a dish in a single layer, with the meatiest portions towards the outside.

Cover and cook on HIGH for 10 minutes, rotating the dish after 5 minutes if the oven does not have a turntable.

Meanwhile, heat the oil in a frying pan, add the onion and green pepper and fry conventionally until golden. Stir in the paprika, tomato purée, tomatoes, stock, and salt and pepper to taste. Bring to the boil and pour over the chicken.

Cover and cook on HIGH for about 20 minutes or until the chicken is tender. Leave to stand, covered, for 5 minutes, then stir in the yogurt.

Garnish with parsley and serve with a green salad.

Serves 4 to 6

CHICKEN À LA KING

50 g (2 oz) butter
2 tablespoons chopped green pepper
2 tablespoons chopped red pepper
2 tablespoons plain flour
milk
1 × 298 g (10½ oz) can condensed cream of chicken soup
350–500 g (12 oz–1 lb) cooked chicken, cubed
2 tablespoons dry white wine
1 × 213 g (7½ oz) can button mushrooms, drained and halved
salt and pepper
French bread, sliced and toasted

Put the butter and peppers into a casserole, cover and cook on HIGH for 2 minutes. Stir in the flour until smooth.

Add enough milk to the soup to make 450 ml (¾ pint) then blend into the flour mixture.

Cook on HIGH for 5½ to 7½ minutes or until thickened, stirring occasionally.

Stir in the remaining ingredients, except the bread with salt and pepper to taste, and cook on HIGH for 2½ to 3½ minutes or until heated through.

Arrange the French bread on warmed individual serving plates and spoon the chicken mixture on top.

Serves 4

MARINATED RABBIT

1 kg (2 lb) rabbit joints
salt and pepper
1 onion, sliced
300 ml (½ pint) dry white wine
300 ml (½ pint) chicken stock
1 bay leaf
1 teaspoon cornflour
12 cocktail silverskin onions
12 stuffed green olives, sliced
1 × 213 g (7½ oz) can button mushrooms, drained and halved
parsley sprig to garnish

Rub the rabbit joints with salt and pepper and put into a dish with the onion, wine, stock and bay leaf. Cover and leave to marinate in the refrigerator overnight.

Discard the onion and bay leaf. Transfer the rabbit and marinade to a casserole, cover and cook on HIGH for 15 to 20 minutes or until tender. Remove the rabbit and set aside.

Blend the cornflour with a little water and stir into the casserole, cover and bring to the boil on HIGH, stirring frequently. Stir in the onions, olives and mushrooms and return the rabbit to the casserole.

Cover and cook on HIGH for 2 to 3 minutes, until heated through. Leave to stand, covered for 5 minutes.

Garnish with parsley and serve with boiled potatoes and buttered mashed swedes.

Serves 4

Marinated Rabbit

CHICKEN CACCIATORE

1 × 397 g (14 oz) can tomatoes
1 × 142 g (5 oz) can tomato purée
120 ml (4 fl oz) dry white wine
1 clove garlic, crushed
1 teaspoon dried oregano
salt
4–6 chicken portions
1 large onion, sliced
TO GARNISH:
lemon twists
parsley sprigs

Put the tomatoes with their juice, tomato purée, wine, garlic, oregano, and salt to taste into a jug and mix well.

Arrange the chicken portions in a casserole, skin side down and meatiest portions towards the outside of the dish. Add the onion rings and pour over the tomato mixture.

Cover and cook on HIGH for 15 minutes. Turn the chicken portions over, rearrange, cover and cook on HIGH for 10 to 15 minutes, until the chicken is tender and the juices run clear. Leave to stand, covered, for 5 minutes.

Garnish with lemon twists and parsley sprigs. Serve with boiled rice.
Serves 4 to 6

(Picture, page 88)

PIQUANT PORK CHOPS

4 loin pork chops, 1 cm ($\frac{1}{2}$ inch) thick
Worcestershire sauce
125 g (4 oz) red Cheddar or Cheshire cheese, grated
2 tablespoons single cream
1 tablespoon Dijon mustard
chopped chives to garnish

Brush the chops sparingly on both sides with Worcestershire sauce. Arrange in a single layer in a dish, with the meatiest portions towards the outside.

Cover and cook on HIGH for 5 minutes. Reduce to LOW and continue cooking for 20 to 22 minutes, draining the chops after 10 minutes.

Mix together the cheese, cream and mustard and spread over the chops. Cook on HIGH for about 2 minutes or until the cheese has melted.

Sprinkle with chopped chives and serve immediately with sauté potatoes and broccoli spears.
Serves 4

JACKET POTATOES WITH SOURED CREAM

4 potatoes
4 knobs of butter
4 tablespoons soured cream
2 teaspoons chopped chives
salt and pepper

Prick the potatoes with a fork and arrange in a circle on kitchen paper in the oven. Cook on HIGH for 6 minutes. Turn the potatoes over, rearrange if the oven does not have a turntable, and cook on HIGH for 7 to 8 minutes. Wrap each potato in foil and leave to stand for 5 minutes.

Unwrap the potatoes, cut a slice off the top of each and carefully scoop out the flesh. Mix with the butter, soured cream, chives, and salt and pepper to taste and pile the mixture back into the potato cases. Reheat on HIGH for 2 to 3 minutes before serving.
Serves 4

STUFFED COURGETTES

2 courgettes, cut in half lengthways
40 g ($1\frac{1}{2}$ oz) easy cook rice
2 tablespoons boiling chicken stock
1 teaspoon chopped parsley
salt and pepper
$\frac{1}{2}$ × 177 g (6 oz) can crabmeat, drained
paprika
parsley sprigs to garnish

Scoop the pulp from the courgettes, leaving a 1 cm ($\frac{1}{2}$ inch) shell. Chop the pulp coarsely and put into a casserole with the rice, stock, parsley, and salt and pepper to taste. Mix well, cover and cook on HIGH for 4 to 6 minutes, until the rice is tender and the moisture has been absorbed.

Stir in the crabmeat and spoon the mixture into the courgette shells. Place in a shallow dish and sprinkle with paprika. Cover with greaseproof paper and cook on HIGH for 4 to 5 minutes or until the shells are tender; rotate the dish after 2 minutes if the oven does not have a turntable. Leave to stand, covered, for 2 to 3 minutes before serving.

Garnish with parsley, and serve with Tomato Sauce (see page 75), if liked.
Serves 4

NOTE: This dish can be served as a starter or, if you double the quantities, it makes a quick supper.

BROAD BEAN MEDLEY

2 tablespoons oil
1 clove garlic, crushed
1 onion, finely chopped
500 g (1 lb) shelled broad beans
350 g (12 oz) tomatoes, skinned and roughly chopped
1 teaspoon caster sugar
½ teaspoon oregano
2 tablespoons wine vinegar
salt and pepper

Put the oil, garlic and onion into a casserole, cover and cook on HIGH for 2 minutes. Stir in the beans, mixing well. Stir in the remaining ingredients, with salt and pepper to taste. Cover and cook on HIGH for 8 to 10 minutes or until the broad beans are tender.

Serves 4

BROCCOLI AND CAULIFLOWER CHEESE

1 × 227 g (8 oz) pack frozen broccoli spears
1 × 227 g (8 oz) pack frozen cauliflower florets
2 tablespoons water
1 packet cheese sauce mix
250 ml (8 fl oz) milk
25 g (1 oz) butter
25 g (1 oz) dry breadcrumbs
chopped parsley to garnish

Put the broccoli, cauliflower and water into a casserole. Cover and cook on HIGH for 10 to 12 minutes or until tender, stirring once or twice during cooking. Drain and return to the dish. Cover and set aside.

Blend the cheese sauce mix with the milk in a Pyrex measure. Cook on HIGH for about 3 minutes or until thickened, stirring every minute.

Melt the butter in a small dish on HIGH for 15 to 30 seconds and stir in the breadcrumbs.

Pour the cheese sauce over the vegetables and sprinkle with the buttered breadcrumbs. If necessary, reheat on HIGH for about 2 minutes before serving, sprinkled with chopped parsley.

Serves 4 to 6

Broad Bean Medley; Broccoli and Cauliflower Cheese

CAULIFLOWER POLONAISE

50 g (2 oz) butter
50 g (2 oz) coarse dry breadcrumbs
1 cauliflower, broken into florets
2 tablespoons water
1 tablespoon finely chopped parsley
2 hard-boiled eggs, finely chopped

Melt the butter in a bowl on HIGH for 1 minute. Stir in the breadcrumbs and set aside.

Put the cauliflower and water into a casserole, cover and cook on HIGH for 8 to 10 minutes or until tender. Drain thoroughly.

Mix the buttered crumbs with the parsley and eggs and sprinkle over the cauliflower to serve.

Serves 4

PEAS BONNE FEMME

125 g (4 oz) streaky bacon, derinded and diced
25 g (1 oz) butter
500 g (1 lb) frozen peas
6 small white button onions
120 ml (4 fl oz) water
salt and pepper
15 g ($\frac{1}{2}$ oz) caster sugar
10 small lettuce leaves

Put the bacon into a casserole, cover with kitchen paper and cook on HIGH for 3 to 4 minutes.

Add the butter, peas, onions, water, and salt and pepper to taste. Cover and cook on HIGH for 8 minutes, stirring after 4 minutes.

Stir in the sugar and lettuce leaves, cover and cook on HIGH for 2 minutes or until the peas and onions are tender.

Serves 4 to 6

BEAN AND POTATO PIE

1 × 447 g ($15\frac{3}{4}$ oz) can beans in tomato sauce
1 kg (2 lb) freshly cooked hot potatoes, sliced
250 g (8 oz) Cheddar cheese, grated
salt and pepper

Spoon half the beans into a casserole. Cover with half the potatoes and sprinkle half the grated cheese on top. Season with salt and pepper to taste. Spoon the remaining beans on top and cover with the remaining potato. Cover and cook on HIGH for 4 minutes or until heated through.

Sprinkle with the remaining cheese, cover and heat for a further 1 to 2 minutes or until the cheese has melted.

Serve as a light lunch or supper dish.

Serves 4

GREEN BEANS WITH ALMONDS

500 g (1 lb) green beans
2 tablespoons water
25 g (1 oz) butter, flaked
25 g (1 oz) flaked almonds
salt and pepper

Put the beans and water into a dish, cover and cook on HIGH for 8 to 10 minutes or until just tender.

Stir in the remaining ingredients, season with salt and pepper to taste, cover and cook on HIGH for 1 minute until the butter has melted. Leave to stand, covered, for 2 minutes before serving.

Serves 4

ROQUEFORT CABBAGE

500 g (1 lb) cabbage, quartered and cored
4 tablespoons water
8 tablespoons Roquefort Dressing (see page 91)

Put the cabbage into a casserole dish with the core ends towards the centre. Add the water, cover and cook on HIGH for 10 minutes or until tender. Leave to stand, covered, for 2 minutes.

Drain and place in a warmed serving dish. Top with the dressing.

Serves 4

HONEY-GLAZED CARROTS

500 g (1 lb) carrots, sliced
4 tablespoons water
15 g (½ oz) butter
pinch of ground cinnamon
1 tablespoon clear honey
TO GARNISH:
2 tablespoons chopped walnuts

Put the carrots and water into a casserole. Cover and cook on HIGH for 10 to 12 minutes or until tender, stirring once. Leave to stand, covered, for 2 minutes.

Stir in the butter and cinnamon, drizzle over the honey and mix gently. Cover and cook on HIGH for 30 seconds. Sprinkle with the walnuts to serve.

Serves 4

LEFT: *Cauliflower Polonaise; Peas Bonne Femme; Bean and Potato Pie*
RIGHT: *Green Beans with Almonds; Roquefort Cabbage; Honey-glazed Carrots*

BRAISED CELERY

1 head of celery, divided into sticks and halved
150 ml (¼ pint) boiling chicken stock
salt and pepper
25 g (1 oz) butter, flaked

Put the celery sticks into a shallow dish with the stock, and salt and pepper to taste. Dot with butter, cover and cook on HIGH for about 12 minutes or until tender; rearrange the celery halfway through cooking. Leave to stand, covered, for 2 to 3 minutes before serving.

Serves 4

SPAGHETTI BOLOGNESE

500 g (1 lb) minced beef
1 onion, chopped
3 tablespoons chopped green pepper
1 × 397 g (14 oz) can tomatoes, drained and cut into large pieces
6 tablespoons tomato purée
4 tablespoons red wine or water
1 bay leaf
2 teaspoons dried oregano
1 teaspoon dried basil
1 tablespoon Worcestershire sauce
1 tablespoon oil
salt
350 g (12 oz) spaghetti
grated Parmesan cheese

Put the minced beef, onion and green pepper into a casserole, stirring to break up the beef. Cover and cook on HIGH for 5 to 6 minutes, stirring twice. Pour off excess juices.

Stir in the tomatoes, tomato purée, wine, bay leaf, oregano, basil and Worcestershire sauce. Cover and cook on HIGH for 12 minutes, stirring twice. Reduce the power to MEDIUM and cook for a further 5 minutes, stirring twice.

Meanwhile, add the oil to a pan of boiling salted water and cook the spaghetti for 10 to 12 minutes, until *al dente*. Drain and transfer to a warmed serving dish.

Pour over the meat sauce, discarding the bay leaf, and sprinkle with Parmesan cheese to serve.

Serves 4

APPLE AND BACON SUPPER

500 g (1 lb) onions, sliced
2 tablespoons water
500 g (1 lb) cooking apples, peeled, cored and sliced
pepper
350 g (12 oz) streaky bacon, derinded

Put the onions and water into a casserole, cover and cook on HIGH for 8 minutes or until tender.

Stir in the apple slices and pepper to taste. Cover and cook on HIGH for 3 minutes, stirring once. Set aside.

Meanwhile, place the bacon on a microwave roasting rack, or between layers of kitchen paper, in a dish and cook on HIGH for 5 to 6 minutes, pouring off excess fat every 2 minutes.

Crumble the bacon and stir into the onion and apple mixture. Cover and cook on HIGH for 2 minutes or until heated through.

Serves 4

HAM AND VEGETABLE PILAU

250 g (8 oz) carrots, thinly sliced
250 g (8 oz) cauliflower florets
125 g (4 oz) leeks, thinly sliced
25 g (1 oz) butter
250 g (8 oz) long-grain rice
½ teaspoon ground cardamom
½ teaspoon paprika
½ teaspoon turmeric (optional)
600 ml (1 pint) chicken stock
125 g (4 oz) cooked ham, cut into strips
1 tablespoon chopped parsley

Put the vegetables and butter into a casserole, cover and cook on HIGH for 5 minutes. Add the rice, spices and stock, cover and cook on HIGH for 7 to 8 minutes.

Reduce the setting to LOW and cook for 15 minutes, stirring occasionally. Stir in the ham and cook on HIGH for 2 to 3 minutes to heat through.

Sprinkle with the parsley to serve.

Serves 4

DEVILLED KIDNEYS

plain flour for coating
salt and pepper
8 lambs' kidneys, skinned, halved and cored
25 g (1 oz) butter
1 small onion, chopped
1 tablespoon Worcestershire sauce
1 tablespoon dry sherry
1 tablespoon chopped parsley
TO GARNISH:
2–3 rounds of fried bread
parsley sprig

Season the flour with salt and pepper and use to coat the kidneys.

Melt the butter in a shallow dish on HIGH for 1 minute. Add the onion, cover and cook on HIGH for 1½ minutes. Stir in the kidneys, cover and cook on HIGH for 4 minutes, stirring after 2 minutes.

Stir in the Worcestershire sauce, sherry and parsley, cover and cook on HIGH for 2 to 3 minutes. Leave to stand for 5 minutes. Serve, garnished with parsley, on rounds of fried bread.

Serves 2

Ham and Vegetable Pilau; Spaghetti Bolognese; Devilled Kidneys

MACKEREL IN GOOSEBERRY SAUCE

50 g (2 oz) butter
75 g (3 oz) fresh breadcrumbs
2 tablespoons chopped parsley
2 tablespoons finely chopped red pepper
1 teaspoon dried basil
2 teaspoons lemon juice
salt and pepper
2 mackerel, cleaned, head and tails removed
1 × 283 g (10 oz) can gooseberries
TO GARNISH:
lemon twists
parsley sprigs

Melt the butter in a bowl on HIGH for 1 minute. Stir in the breadcrumbs, parsley, red pepper, basil, lemon juice, and salt and pepper to taste and mix well to form the stuffing.

Fill the mackerel cavities with the stuffing. Arrange in a dish and make 3 slits in the skin of each fish.

Put the gooseberries with their juice into an electric blender or food processor and work until smooth. Pour over the fish.

Cover and cook on HIGH for 7 minutes. Leave to stand for 2 to 3 minutes. Garnish with lemon twists and parsley and serve with boiled new potatoes.

Serves 2

MOCK LASAGNE

1 × 227 g (8 oz) packet frozen chopped spinach
500 g (1 lb) minced beef
1 teaspoon garlic salt
1 × 397 g (14 oz) can tomatoes, liquidized or sieved
4 tablespoons dry breadcrumbs
1 × 227 g (8 oz) carton cottage cheese
1 egg, beaten
pepper
125 g (4 oz) Mozzarella cheese, sliced
2 tablespoons grated Parmesan cheese

Put the spinach into a small dish. Cover and cook on HIGH for 3 minutes or until defrosted. Drain well and set aside.

Put the minced beef into a casserole, stirring to break it up, and sprinkle with the garlic salt. Cook on HIGH for 5 to 6 minutes or until browned, stirring after 2 minutes. Drain off excess juices. Stir in the tomatoes, cover and cook on HIGH for about 1 minute, until bubbling. Stir in half the breadcrumbs.

Put the spinach, cottage cheese, egg, remaining breadcrumbs, and pepper to taste into a bowl; mix well.

Spread half the meat mixture in a 23 cm (9 inch) square dish. Cover with the spinach mixture then the Mozzarella cheese. Top with the remaining meat and sprinkle with the Parmesan cheese.

Cook on HIGH for 4 minutes, rotate the dish if the oven does not have a turntable, and cook on HIGH for a further 4 minutes. Leave to stand for 5 minutes before serving.

Serves 4

LEFT: *Mackerel in Gooseberry Sauce*
RIGHT: *Chocolate Rum Gâteau; Madeleines*

MICROWAVE SHORT CUTS FOR DESSERTS

Time and time again, the microwave pays dividends when it comes to speeding up traditional cooking processes.

To melt chocolate for desserts and cake recipes, break 50 g (2 oz) into small pieces and place in a glass bowl or jug and cook on MEDIUM for 2–2½ minutes. Do not heat chocolate on full power as this can cause it to overheat.

Gelatine is easy to dissolve in the microwave. Sprinkle 1 sachet of powdered gelatine over the liquid recommended in the recipe, leave until spongy and then cook on HIGH for 30 seconds. Allow to cool slightly before adding all the other ingredients.

CHOCOLATE RUM GÂTEAU

1 tablespoon cocoa powder
2 tablespoons boiling water
125 g (4 oz) soft margarine
125 g (4 oz) caster sugar
125 g (4 oz) self-raising flour, sifted
1 teaspoon baking powder
2 eggs, beaten

CHOCOLATE SYRUP:

125 g (4 oz) granulated sugar
1 tablespoon cocoa powder
150 ml ($\frac{1}{4}$ pint) water
2 tablespoons rum

TO DECORATE:

1 × 284 ml ($\frac{1}{2}$ pint) carton double cream
1 tablespoon milk
chocolate leaves

Blend the cocoa and water together until smooth; leave to cool. Put into a mixing bowl with the remaining cake ingredients and beat until smooth.

Spoon into a 23 cm (9 inch) microwave ring mould and level the top. Cook on HIGH for 4 to 5 minutes. Leave to stand for 10 minutes, then turn onto a wire rack to cool.

Meanwhile, make the syrup. Put the sugar, cocoa and water into a bowl and cook on HIGH for $1\frac{1}{2}$ to 2 minutes, until dissolved. Cool and stir in the rum.

Return the cake to the ring mould, pour over the syrup and leave to soak for 10 to 15 minutes.

Whip the cream and milk together. Place the cake on a serving plate, cover with the cream and decorate with chocolate leaves.

Serves 6 to 8

MADELEINES

125 g (4 oz) soft margarine
125 g (4 oz) caster sugar
2 eggs, beaten
125 g (4 oz) self-raising flour, sifted
6 tablespoons raspberry jam
desiccated coconut to cover
6 glacé cherry halves to decorate

Put the margarine, sugar, eggs and flour into a mixing bowl and beat together until light and fluffy. Divide the mixture equally between 6 paper drinking cups.

Arrange in a circle in the oven and cook on HIGH for about $3\frac{1}{2}$ minutes, rearranging the cups after $1\frac{1}{2}$ minutes and removing any which are cooked sooner. Flex the cups and turn the cakes onto a wire rack to cool.

Put the raspberry jam into a small bowl and heat on HIGH for 30 to 40 seconds, stirring after 15 seconds. Brush the cold cakes with warmed jam and roll them in the coconut to coat. Place a glacé cherry half on top of each to decorate.

Makes 6

RASPBERRY CREAM GÂTEAU

150 g (5 oz) self-raising flour
25 g (1 oz) cornflour
pinch of salt
150 g (5 oz) caster sugar
2 eggs, separated
4 tablespoons warm water
2 tablespoons corn oil
few drops of vanilla essence
TO FINISH:
350 g (12 oz) frozen raspberries, thawed
1 × 284 ml (½ pint) carton double cream, whipped

Sift the flour, cornflour, salt and sugar into a bowl. Beat the egg yolks and stir in the water, oil and vanilla essence. Stir into the dry ingredients. Whisk the egg whites until stiff and fold into the mixture.

Divide between two lined and greased 18 cm (7 inch) cake dishes. Cook one at a time on HIGH for about 4 minutes. Leave to stand for 5 minutes before turning out onto a wire rack to cool. Chill for 1 hour.

Cut each sponge in half. Sandwich the layers together with raspberries and cream, reserving some for the top.

Serves 8

Raspberry Cream Gâteau

PINEAPPLE À LA CRÈME

1 × 439 g (15½ oz) can pineapple pieces in natural juice, drained with juice reserved
50 g (2 oz) cornflour
3 tablespoons caster sugar or to taste
few drops of vanilla essence
1 × 284 ml (½ pint) carton double cream, whipped

Make up the pineapple juice to 600 ml (1 pint) with water, and pour into a large serving bowl. Blend in the cornflour, then stir in the sugar. Cook on HIGH for 6 minutes, stirring frequently. Stir in the vanilla essence and leave to cool.

Reserve 5 tablespoons of the cream and fold the remainder into the cornflour mixture. Fold in the pineapple, reserving a few pieces for decoration. Chill until set. Decorate with cream rosettes and pineapple.

Serves 4

CHOCOLATE MOUSSE

125 g (4 oz) plain chocolate, broken into small pieces
15 g (½ oz) butter, softened
4 eggs, separated
1 tablespoon rum
TO DECORATE:
120 ml (4 fl oz) whipping cream, whipped

Put the chocolate pieces into a bowl with the butter. Cook on HIGH for 2 minutes until melted, stirring after 1 minute. Stir in the beaten egg yolks and rum. Whisk the egg whites until stiff and fold into the mixture. Pour into 4 to 6 individual dishes and chill until set.

Decorate with whipped cream.

Serves 4 to 6

BAKED STUFFED APPLES

4 cooking apples, cored
4 tablespoons mincemeat
4 tablespoons apple juice (optional)

Prick the skins of the apples with a fork and arrange in a circle on a dish.

Fill the cavities with mincemeat and drizzle with the apple juice, if using. Cover and cook on HIGH for 7 to 9 minutes, depending on size, until almost tender. Leave to stand, covered, for 5 minutes.

Spoon over the juices and serve with whipped cream.

Serves 4

APRICOT CRUNCH

50 g (2 oz) butter
50 g (2 oz) soft dark brown sugar
50 g (2 oz) porridge oats
50 g (2 oz) plain flour
1 × 397 g (14 oz) can apricot pie filling
1 tablespoon demerara sugar
2 tablespoons crunchnut topping or mixed chopped nuts

Melt the butter in a bowl on HIGH for 45 to 60 seconds. Stir in the soft brown sugar and oats. Cook on HIGH for 2 minutes.

Stir in the sifted flour, using a knife to cut into the mixture, until it resembles coarse breadcrumbs.

Put the apricot pie filling into the base of a greased 900 ml ($1\frac{1}{2}$ pint) pie dish and cover with the oat mixture. Sprinkle with the demerara sugar and crunchnut topping or nuts.

Cook on HIGH for 8 to 10 minutes, rotating the dish halfway during cooking if the oven does not have a turntable.

Serve warm with cream.

Serves 4

COFFEE MARBLE CROWN

125 g (4 oz) self-raising flour
125 g (4 oz) soft margarine
125 g (4 oz) caster sugar
2 eggs, beaten
1 tablespoon milk
3 teaspoons instant coffee powder or granules
120 ml (4 fl oz) warm water

TO FINISH:

1 kiwi fruit, sliced
1 nectarine, sliced
few strawberries, sliced
few seedless grapes
1 × 142 ml (5 fl oz) carton double or whipping cream, whipped

Sift the flour into a bowl, add the margarine, sugar, eggs and milk and beat well.

Turn into a 23 cm (9 inch) microwave ring mould and cook on HIGH for 4 minutes. Leave to stand for 2 to 3 minutes, then turn onto a wire rack to cool.

Mix the coffee powder or granules with the water in a small bowl and heat on HIGH for 1 minute.

Return the cooled cake to the ring mould and pour over the coffee. Leave to soak for 30 minutes.

Turn out onto a serving plate and fill the centre with the fruit. Pipe cream around the top and side to decorate.

Serves 6 to 8

JAM SPONGE PUDDING

125 g (4 oz) margarine
125 g (4 oz) caster sugar
2 eggs, beaten
125 g (4 oz) plain flour
1 teaspoon baking powder
1 tablespoon warm water
3 tablespoons jam

Cream the margarine and sugar together until light and fluffy. Beat in the eggs, then fold in the sifted flour, baking powder and water.

Put the jam into the base of a 900 ml ($1\frac{1}{2}$ pint) pudding basin lined with cling film, and heat on HIGH for 30 seconds.

Add the sponge mixture, cover and cook on HIGH for about 6 minutes. Leave to stand for 5 minutes, before turning out to serve.

Serves 4 to 6

Jam Sponge Pudding; Apricot Crunch

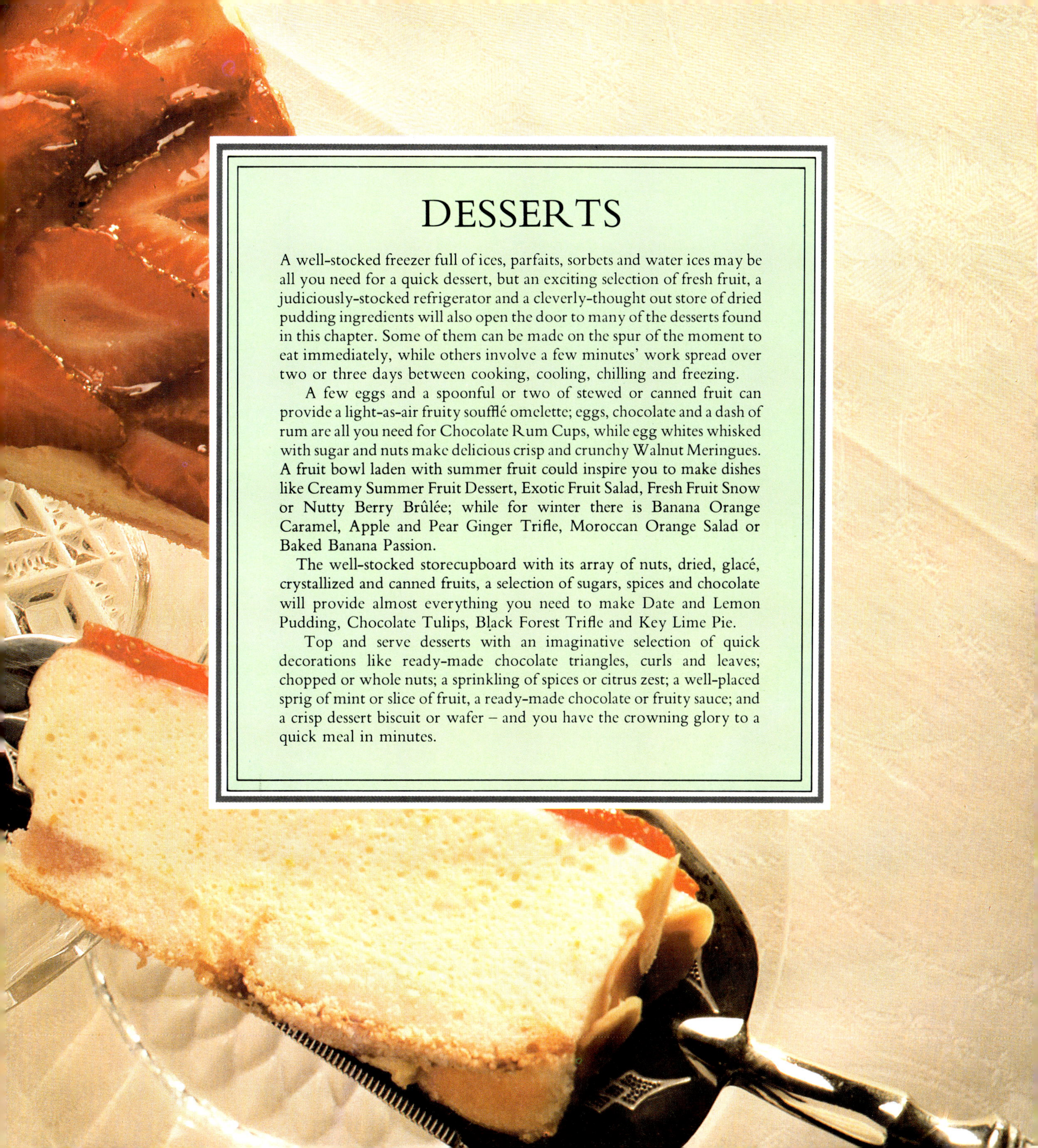

DESSERTS

A well-stocked freezer full of ices, parfaits, sorbets and water ices may be all you need for a quick dessert, but an exciting selection of fresh fruit, a judiciously-stocked refrigerator and a cleverly-thought out store of dried pudding ingredients will also open the door to many of the desserts found in this chapter. Some of them can be made on the spur of the moment to eat immediately, while others involve a few minutes' work spread over two or three days between cooking, cooling, chilling and freezing.

A few eggs and a spoonful or two of stewed or canned fruit can provide a light-as-air fruity soufflé omelette; eggs, chocolate and a dash of rum are all you need for Chocolate Rum Cups, while egg whites whisked with sugar and nuts make delicious crisp and crunchy Walnut Meringues. A fruit bowl laden with summer fruit could inspire you to make dishes like Creamy Summer Fruit Dessert, Exotic Fruit Salad, Fresh Fruit Snow or Nutty Berry Brûlée; while for winter there is Banana Orange Caramel, Apple and Pear Ginger Trifle, Moroccan Orange Salad or Baked Banana Passion.

The well-stocked storecupboard with its array of nuts, dried, glacé, crystallized and canned fruits, a selection of sugars, spices and chocolate will provide almost everything you need to make Date and Lemon Pudding, Chocolate Tulips, Black Forest Trifle and Key Lime Pie.

Top and serve desserts with an imaginative selection of quick decorations like ready-made chocolate triangles, curls and leaves; chopped or whole nuts; a sprinkling of spices or citrus zest; a well-placed sprig of mint or slice of fruit, a ready-made chocolate or fruity sauce; and a crisp dessert biscuit or wafer – and you have the crowning glory to a quick meal in minutes.

BERRY SOUFFLÉ OMELETTE

6 tablespoons stewed raspberries
6 eggs, separated
3 tablespoons caster sugar
3 tablespoons water
pinch of salt
TO DECORATE:
few fresh raspberries
sifted icing sugar

Place the raspberries in a greased shallow ovenproof dish.

Whisk the egg yolks and sugar together until pale. Stir in the water.

Whisk the egg whites with the salt until stiff, then fold into the egg yolks. Pour over the raspberries and cook in a preheated moderate oven, 180°C (350°F), Gas Mark 4, for about 25 to 30 minutes. Top with the raspberries and sprinkle with icing sugar.

Serves 4

NUTTY BERRY BRÛLÉE

500 g (1 lb) gooseberries
50–125 g (2–4 oz) caster sugar
300 g (10 oz) hazelnut yogurt
2 tablespoons soft dark brown sugar

Place the gooseberries in a saucepan with caster sugar to taste. Cook gently, stirring, until the juices run, then cover and simmer until tender.

Spoon into individual heatproof dishes and leave to cool. Top with the yogurt and chill well.

Just before serving, sprinkle with brown sugar and place under a preheated hot grill for 1 to 2 minutes. Serve immediately.

Serves 4

DATE AND LEMON PUDDING

6 slices buttered wholemeal bread, crusts removed and quartered
75 g (3 oz) dates, stoned and chopped
2 eggs
4 tablespoons soft light brown sugar
2 teaspoons finely grated lemon rind
½ teaspoon ground mixed spice
600 ml (1 pint) milk

Arrange the bread in a greased 600 ml (1 pint) ovenproof dish. Sprinkle the dates over the top.

Beat together the egg, 1 tablespoon of the sugar, the lemon rind and spice. Heat the milk, but do not boil; stir into the egg mixture.

Strain the custard over the bread and leave for 10 to 15 minutes. Stand the dish in a roasting pan, containing enough water to come halfway up the dish. Cook in a preheated moderate oven, 180°C (350°F), Gas Mark 4, for about 40 minutes or until the custard is just set.

Sprinkle with the remaining sugar and serve immediately.

Serves 4

SPICED APPLE AMBER

500 g (1 lb) cooking apples, peeled, cored and sliced
4 teaspoons clear honey
½ teaspoon ground cinnamon
½ teaspoon grated nutmeg
2 tablespoons water
2 eggs, separated
50 g (2 oz) caster sugar

Place the apples, honey, cinnamon, nutmeg and water in a saucepan. Heat gently until the apples are tender. Cool slightly, then sieve or purée in an electric blender. Beat in the egg yolks, then spoon into a buttered 1.2 litre (2 pint) ovenproof dish.

Whisk the egg whites until stiff, then whisk in half the sugar. Fold in the remainder and spoon over the apples.

Cook in a preheated moderate oven, 180°C (350°F), Gas Mark 4, for about 15 to 20 minutes. Serve hot, with cream.

Serves 4

LEFT: *Berry Soufflé Omelette; Nutty Berry Brûlée*
RIGHT: *Banana Splits with Fudge Sauce*

BANANA SPLITS WITH FUDGE SAUCE

4 bananas
8 tablespoons vanilla ice cream
8 tablespoons double cream, whipped
4 teaspoons chopped nuts
2 glacé cherries, halved

SAUCE:
25 g (1 oz) plain chocolate
2 tablespoons warm water
125 g (4 oz) soft light brown sugar
2 teaspoons golden syrup
4–6 drops vanilla essence

Cut the bananas in half lengthways and sandwich the halves together with the ice cream. Place on individual serving places. Spoon or pipe the cream on top and decorate with the nuts and cherry pieces.

To make the sauce: Melt the chocolate with the water in a basin standing over a pan of hot water.

Transfer to a saucepan and add the sugar and syrup. Heat gently, stirring, until the sugar has dissolved. Bring to the boil and boil steadily, without stirring, for 3 to 4 minutes. Remove from the heat and stir in the vanilla.

Pour the sauce over the banana splits or hand separately.

Serves 4

CHOCOLATE TULIPS

TULIP BASKETS:
2 egg whites
125 g (4 oz) caster sugar
50 g (2 oz) butter, melted
50 g (2 oz) plain flour
CHOCOLATE CREAM:
75 g (3 oz) plain chocolate, chopped
2 tablespoons whipping cream
$\frac{1}{2} \times 439$ g ($15\frac{1}{2}$ oz) can unsweetened chestnut purée
1 tablespoon caster sugar
2 tablespoons brandy
TO DECORATE:
8 chocolate triangles or chocolate leaves

Whisk the egg whites in a bowl until stiff but not dry then gradually whisk in the caster sugar, a little at a time. Pour the butter around the side of the bowl then sift the flour over the mixture. Using a metal spoon fold them into the meringue mixture.

Place 3 tablespoons of the mixture on a baking sheet lined with silicone paper and spread to form a 13 cm (5 inch) round. Repeat with the remaining mixture to make 8 rounds.

Bake in a preheated moderately hot oven 190°C (375°F), Gas Mark 5, for 8–10 minutes or until the edges are golden.

Leave to cool slightly, then remove with a plastic spatula and place each one top side down over the base of an inverted glass, moulding to give wavy edges. Leave to set, then remove carefully. Repeat with the remaining rounds.

Heat the chocolate and cream in a small pan gently until melted. Leave to cool.

Blend the chestnut purée, sugar, chocolate and brandy in a blender or food processor until smooth.

Place the mixture in a piping bag, fitted with a large fluted nozzle, and pipe into the tulip cases. Decorate each one with a chocolate triangle or leaf.

Serves 8

NOTE: The tulip baskets and the chocolate cream can both be made the day before. Store the tulip baskets in an airtight container and keep the chocolate cream in the refrigerator until required.

CHOCOLATE MOUSSE

175 g (6 oz) cooking chocolate, broken into pieces
3 tablespoons strong black coffee
1 tablespoon brandy
4 eggs, separated
TO DECORATE:
1 × 142 ml (5 fl oz) carton double cream, whipped
flaked almonds, toasted

Put the chocolate, coffee and brandy into a bowl over a saucepan of hot water and stir until melted. Remove from the heat and leave to cool for 1 minute.

Add the egg yolks to the chocolate mixture and beat well. Whisk the egg whites until stiff and fold into the chocolate mixture.

Pour into a soufflé dish and chill for at least 3 hours before serving. Decorate with whipped cream and almonds.

Serves 4

CHOCOLATE AND ORANGE MOUSSE

125 g (4 oz) plain chocolate
knob of butter
grated rind and juice of 1 orange
2 eggs, separated
142 ml (5 fl oz) double cream, whipped
chocolate curls to decorate

Melt the chocolate in a basin over a pan of hot water. Remove from the heat and add the butter, orange rind and juice, and the egg yolks. Beat until smooth. Leave to cool.

Fold in the whipped cream. Whisk the egg whites until just firm and fold into the chocolate mixture. Pour into individual serving dishes. Chill in the refrigerator until set.

Decorate with the chocolate curls before serving.

Serves 4

Chocolate Tulips

CHOCOLATE SYLLABUB

125 g (4 oz) plain chocolate, broken into pieces
3 tablespoons brandy
284 ml (10 fl oz) double cream, whipped
2 egg whites
grated chocolate to decorate

Place the chocolate and brandy in a small saucepan and heat very gently until melted. Stir until smooth, then leave to cool.

Whisk the cream into the cooled chocolate.

Whisk the egg whites in a bowl until they stand in soft peaks then carefully fold them into the chocolate mixture.

Spoon into individual glasses and sprinkle with grated chocolate or chocolate curls.

Serves 4

CHOCOLATE WHISKY CREAMS

142 ml (5 fl oz) single cream
125 g (4 oz) plain chocolate, finely chopped
2 small egg yolks
2 tablespoons whisky
TO DECORATE:
1 small egg white
6 tablespoons double cream, whipped
4 chocolate leaves

Place the cream in a saucepan and heat to just below boiling point. Pour into an electric blender or food processor, add the chocolate and egg yolks and blend for 30 seconds. Add the whisky and blend for 10 seconds. Pour into 4 individual glasses and chill until set.

Whisk the egg white until stiff, fold carefully into the whipped cream then pile on top of the chocolate mixture. Decorate each serving with a chocolate leaf.

Serves 4

CHOCOLATE RUM CUPS

75 g (3 oz) plain chocolate, melted
RUM FILLING:
1 egg, separated
2 teaspoons rum
25 g (1 oz) plain chocolate, melted
chocolate curls to decorate

Spread the chocolate around the inside of 4 individual paper cake cases. Chill until set hard, then carefully peel away the paper to make 4 chocolate cases.

For the filling, add the egg yolk and rum to the melted chocolate and mix well. Whisk the egg white until fairly stiff then carefully fold into the chocolate mixture. Divide the rum filling equally among the chocolate cases.

Chill before serving, decorated with chocolate curls.

Makes 4

LEFT: *Chocolate Syllabub; Chocolate Whisky Creams*
RIGHT: *Chocolate Chiffon Pie; Choc-orange Cream*

CHOCOLATE CHIFFON PIE

50 g (2 oz) butter or margarine, melted
175 g (6 oz) digestive biscuits, crushed
25 g (1 oz) demerara sugar
FILLING:
250 ml (8 fl oz) milk
200 g (7 oz) plain chocolate, broken into pieces
2 eggs, separated
15 g ($\frac{1}{2}$ oz) gelatine, soaked in 3 tablespoons cold water
75 g (3 oz) caster sugar
142 ml (5 fl oz) double cream, whipped
TO DECORATE:
142 ml (5 fl oz) double cream
chocolate triangles

Combine the butter or margarine, biscuit crumbs and demerara sugar. Press over the base and sides of a 20 cm (8 inch) loose-bottomed flan tin. Place in the refrigerator to harden.

Meanwhile, make the filling. Place the milk and chocolate in a saucepan and heat gently until melted. Bring just to the boil, then pour on to the egg yolks. Return to the pan and cook, stirring, until thickened. Add the soaked gelatine and stir until dissolved. Leave until just beginning to set.

Whisk the egg whites until stiff, then gradually whisk in the sugar.

Whisk the chocolate mixture into the cream, then fold in the egg whites. Turn into the crumb case and smooth the surface with a palette knife. Chill until set, then remove from the tin. Decorate with piped whipped cream and chocolate triangles.

Serves 4 to 6

CHOC-ORANGE CREAM

15 g ($\frac{1}{2}$ oz) gelatine
grated rind and juice of 1 orange
600 ml (1 pint) milk
3 tablespoons cornflour
2 tablespoons caster sugar
175 g (6 oz) plain chocolate, broken into pieces
142 ml (5 fl oz) double cream, whipped
2 tablespoons Grand Marnier
4 tablespoons whipped cream to decorate

Soak the gelatine in the orange juice. Blend a little of the milk with the cornflour, and bring the remaining milk to the boil.

Pour the hot milk onto the blended cornflour. Mix well, then return to the pan and add the sugar. Cook, stirring, for 2 to 3 minutes, until thickened, then add the chocolate, orange rind and soaked gelatine and stir over low heat until melted. Leave to cool, stirring occasionally, so no skin forms.

Fold the cream into the mixture, with the Grand Marnier, then turn into a lightly greased 900 ml ($1\frac{1}{2}$ pint) decorative mould and chill until set. Turn out onto a plate and decorate with whipped cream.

Serves 4

APRICOT AND CHOCOLATE DESSERT

4 thick slices chocolate Swiss roll
8 canned apricot halves
150 g (5 oz) apricot yogurt
142 ml (5 fl oz) double cream, whipped
grated chocolate to decorate

Place the Swiss roll in individual serving dishes. Drain the apricots and use a little of the juice to moisten the Swiss roll. Chop the apricots and spoon over the Swiss roll.

Fold the yogurt into the cream, spoon over the apricots and decorate with grated chocolate. Serve chilled.

Serves 4

NOTE: Apricot fromage frais can be used instead of apricot yogurt to make a richer dessert.

BLACKCURRANT SYLLABUB

250 g (8 oz) blackcurrants
50 g (2 oz) granulated sugar
grated rind and juice of 1 lemon
2 tablespoons sherry
225 ml (8 fl oz) double cream
2 tablespoons caster sugar

Place the blackcurrants, granulated sugar, lemon rind and juice in a saucepan and cook gently for 5 minutes. Cool slightly, then purée in an electric blender or rub through a sieve. Stir in the sherry.

Place the cream, caster sugar and half the blackcurrant purée in a bowl and whisk until the mixture forms soft peaks.

Spoon the remaining purée into the base of 4 glasses and top with the cream mixture. Chill before serving, with sponge fingers, if liked.

Serves 4

APRICOT AND BANANA CREAM

125 g (4 oz) dried apricots
4 ripe bananas
4 teaspoons lemon juice
8 tablespoons double cream
4 tablespoons natural low-fat yogurt
4 teaspoons honey
4 walnut halves to decorate

Place the apricots in a bowl and pour over cold water to cover. Leave to soak for a few hours; drain.

Place the bananas in an electric blender or food processor with the apricots, lemon juice, cream, yogurt and honey. Blend to a smooth cream.

Spoon into individual glass serving dishes and chill before serving. Decorate with walnut halves.

Serves 4

STRAWBERRY MOUSSE

500 g (1 lb) fresh or frozen strawberries, thawed
50 g (2 oz) caster sugar
4 tablespoons water
15 g (½ oz) gelatine
284 ml (10 fl oz) double cream
2 egg whites
TO SERVE:
Raspberry sauce (see box, below)

Place the strawberries and sugar in a blender or food processor and work to a purée.

Put the water into a small saucepan, sprinkle over the gelatine and heat gently until dissolved.

Stir the liquid gelatine into the strawberry purée, then pour in the cream and blend well.

Whisk the egg whites and fold into the mixture. Pour into 4 individual moulds and chill until set.

Turn out onto plates and pour over the raspberry sauce to serve.

Serves 4

BERRY FRUIT SAUCES

These are quick and easy to make and add an extra touch to an ice cream or simple dessert. Place 250 g (8 oz) raspberries or strawberries in a food processor or liquidizer with 25 g (1 oz) caster sugar and 3 tablespoons of sweet white wine and blend until smooth. Serve hot or cold.

LEFT: *Apricot and Chocolate Dessert; Blackcurrant Syllabub*
RIGHT: *Creamy Summer Fruit Dessert*

CREAMY SUMMER FRUIT DESSERT

50 g (2 oz) sugar
8 tablespoons water
350 g (12 oz) red plums, stoned
250 g (8 oz) raspberries
142 ml (5 fl oz) soured cream
4 teaspoons soft light brown sugar

Place the sugar and water in a saucepan and heat gently until dissolved. Increase the heat and boil steadily for 2 minutes. Cool, then chill.

Cut the plums into slices. Divide the plums and raspberries between individual serving dishes and pour over the syrup. Spoon the soured cream over the fruit and sprinkle with brown sugar. Serve chilled.

Serves 4

BANANA ORANGE CARAMEL

2 bananas, sliced
2 pears, peeled, cored and sliced
½ teaspoon ground cinnamon
grated rind and juice of 1 orange
2 tablespoons water
50 g (2 oz) sugar
4 eggs, beaten
toasted almonds to decorate

Place the bananas, pears, cinnamon, orange rind and juice in a saucepan and simmer for 5 minutes. Remove from the heat and leave to cool.

Place the water and sugar in a saucepan and heat gently until dissolved. Bring to the boil and boil steadily until a rich golden brown caramel is formed. Pour into 4 buttered ramekins or individual glass dishes.

Strain the eggs over the fruit and stir well. Pour into the moulds.

Place in a roasting pan containing enough water to come halfway up the dishes. Cook in a preheated cool oven, 150°C (300°F), Gas Mark 2, for 25 to 30 minutes or until just firm.

Leave in the refrigerator overnight. Just before serving, turn out and sprinkle with almonds. Serve with cream.

Serves 4

CRUNCHY APPLES

500 g (1 lb) cooking apples, peeled, cored and sliced
50 g (2 oz) granulated sugar
2 teaspoons lemon juice
2 tablespoons water
½ teaspoon ground cinnamon
40 g (1½ oz) butter
75 g (3 oz) porridge oats
2 tablespoons soft light brown sugar
8 tablespoons double cream
4 teaspoons milk
grated chocolate to decorate

Place the apples in a saucepan with the granulated sugar, lemon juice, water and cinnamon. Cook gently until the fruit is soft. Beat to a pulp with a wooden spoon, then spoon into individual glass serving dishes.

Melt the butter in a saucepan and add the porridge oats and brown sugar. Heat gently, stirring, until the oats are browned; leave to cool. Spoon over the apples.

Whip the cream and milk together lightly and spoon over the topping. Decorate with grated chocolate.

Serves 4

FRESH FRUIT SNOW

500 g (1 lb) raspberries or strawberries
1 tablespoon water
caster sugar
3 egg whites
toasted flaked almonds to decorate

Place the fruit and water in an electric blender or food processor and work to a purée. Spoon into a bowl and sweeten to taste.

Whisk the egg whites until stiff, sprinkle in 1 tablespoon sugar and whisk again. Fold into the fruit purée. Spoon into 4 serving glasses, decorate with the almonds and chill until required.

Serves 4

Crunchy Apples

CITRUS TRIFLES

4 trifle sponges
2 tablespoons Cointreau
2 oranges, peeled and roughly chopped
3 tablespoons lemon curd
2 egg whites
4 lemon twists to decorate

Put the trifle sponges into 4 individual glass dishes and sprinkle with the Cointreau.

Divide the oranges between the trifle sponges.

Put the lemon curd into a bowl. Whisk the egg whites until stiff and fold into the lemon curd. Spoon over the orange pieces.

Decorate with lemon twists. Chill before serving.

Serves 4

BLACK FOREST TRIFLE

1 chocolate Swiss roll
3 tablespoons Kirsch
1 × 425 g (15 oz) can black cherries, drained and stoned
3 egg yolks
1 tablespoon cornflour
25 g (1 oz) caster sugar
450 ml (15 fl oz) milk
¼ teaspoon almond essence
142 ml (5 fl oz) double cream, whipped
fresh black cherries to decorate (optional)

Slice the Swiss roll and arrange in a glass bowl. Sprinkle with the Kirsch and cherries, reserving a few if using for decoration.

Cream the egg yolks with the cornflour and sugar. Bring the milk to the boil, pour onto the egg yolks and stir well. Return to the pan and cook gently, stirring constantly, until the mixture coats the back of a wooden spoon. Add the almond essence, pour over the cherries and leave to cool.

Spread three quarters of the cream over the custard. Pipe the remainder into rosettes over the top. Decorate with fresh or reserved canned cherries.

Serves 4

APPLE AND PEAR GINGER TRIFLE

2 medium cooking apples, peeled, cored and sliced
2 medium pears, peeled, cored and sliced
8 tablespoons cider
50 g (2 oz) soft light brown sugar
½ teaspoon ground ginger
6 slices ginger cake, cut in half
142 ml (5 fl oz) whipping cream
4 teaspoons icing sugar, sifted
2 tablespoons chopped nuts, toasted

Place the apples and pears in a saucepan with the cider, brown sugar and ginger. Cook gently until the fruit is just tender. Leave to cool.

Arrange the cake in 4 individual glass serving dishes and spoon the fruit and cooking liquid over the top.

Lightly whip the cream and fold in the icing sugar. Spoon over the fruit and sprinkle with the nuts. Serve chilled.

Serves 4

Black Forest Trifle

COFFEE JUNKET

600 ml (1 pint) milk
2 teaspoons caster sugar
2 teaspoons instant coffee powder
1 teaspoon rennet essence
4 walnut pieces to decorate

Place the milk, sugar and coffee in a saucepan. Heat gently, stirring to dissolve the coffee and sugar, until the mixture reaches 'blood heat'.

Stir in the rennet and pour into individual serving bowls. Leave at room temperature for $1\frac{1}{2}$ hours or until set.

Chill before serving. Decorate with walnut pieces.

Serves 4

QUICK RHUBARB FOOL

500 g (1 lb) rhubarb, chopped
2 tablespoons water
grated rind of 1 orange
75 g (3 oz) sugar
225 ml (8 fl oz) double cream, whipped
150 g (5 oz) raspberry yogurt

Place the rhubarb in a saucepan with the water, orange rind and sugar. Cook gently until soft. Leave to cool, then purée in an electric blender or rub through a sieve.

Fold two-thirds of the cream into the rhubarb with the yogurt. Spoon into individual glass dishes and pipe whirls of cream on top. Chill before serving.

Serves 4

ORANGE CHEESECAKE

50 g (2 oz) butter
175 g (6 oz) digestive biscuits, crushed
50 g (2 oz) soft light brown sugar

FILLING:
227 g (8 oz) curd cheese
50 g (2 oz) caster sugar
grated rind and juice of 1 orange
225 ml (8 fl oz) double cream, whipped
mandarin oranges to decorate

Melt the butter and stir in the crushed biscuits and brown sugar. Press the mixture over the base and sides of a 20 cm (8 inch) flan dish. Leave in the refrigerator until firm.

Mix the curd cheese with the sugar, orange rind and juice. Fold in two-thirds of the cream. Spoon the mixture into the crumb case.

Decorate with the remaining cream and mandarin oranges. Chill before serving.

Serves 4 to 6

KEY LIME PIE

50 g (2 oz) soft light brown sugar
175 g (6 oz) digestive biscuits, crushed
50 g (2 oz) butter, melted
grated rind and juice of 3 limes
15 g (½ oz) gelatine, dissolved in 2 tablespoons water
2 eggs, separated
few drops of green food colouring (optional)
1 × 397 g (14 oz) can condensed milk
TO DECORATE:
1 lime, thinly sliced
whipped cream

Stir the sugar and biscuit crumbs into the melted butter until well mixed. Turn into a 20 cm (8 inch) pie dish or loose-bottomed flan tin and press evenly over the bottom and sides. Chill well.

Add the lime juice to the dissolved gelatine, then whisk in the grated rind, egg yolks and colouring (if using). Gradually whisk in the condensed milk. Leave until just beginning to set, stirring occasionally.

Whisk the egg whites until really stiff and fold into the lime mixture. Turn into the crumb case and chill for several hours.

Remove from the tin and decorate with lime slices and piped cream rosettes.

Serves 4 to 6

YOGURT WITH DRIED FRUIT

625 g (1¼ lb) natural low-fat yogurt
100 g (4 oz) mixed dried fruit, chopped (apricots, apples, peaches, prunes, etc.)
½ teaspoon ground cinnamon

Mix all the ingredients together in a serving bowl and chill for at least 3 hours.

Serves 4

CHOCOLATE AND RUM CHARLOTTE

1½ packets sponge fingers
4 tablespoons rum
100 g (3½ oz) plain chocolate
75 g (3 oz) soft light brown sugar
125 g (4 oz) unsalted butter, softened
2 eggs, separated
TO DECORATE:
142 ml (5 fl oz) double cream, whipped
chocolate leaves or chocolate curls

Dip each sponge finger into the rum and use to line the base and sides of an 18 cm (6 inch) soufflé dish, sugar side out.

Melt the chocolate in a basin over hot water. Cream the sugar and butter in another bowl until light, then stir in the chocolate while it is still hot. Beat in the egg yolks, then fold in the stiffly whisked egg whites. Pour the mixture into the soufflé dish and chill in the refrigerator for 24 hours.

Before turning out the charlotte, using a sharp knife, carefully trim the sponge fingers to the level of the chocolate filling. Invert the charlotte onto a serving plate and decorate with the whipped cream and chocolate leaves or chocolate curls.

Serves 4 to 6

LEFT: *Coffee Junket; Quick Rhubarb Fool; Orange Cheesecake*
RIGHT: *Chocolate and Rum Charlotte*

GINGER LOG

24 ginger snaps
4 tablespoons rum or brandy
1 × 284 ml (½ pint) carton and 1 × 142 ml (5 fl oz) carton double cream
1½ teaspoons ground ginger
1½ tablespoons caster sugar
1½ tablespoons ginger syrup (from stem ginger)
stem ginger slices to decorate

Place the biscuits in a shallow dish and sprinkle with the rum. Leave until completely absorbed.

Whip the cream with the ground ginger and sugar until stiff. Fold in the ginger syrup.

Sandwich all the biscuits together, using two-thirds of the cream, to make a long roll. Place on a serving dish and cover with the remaining cream. Decorate with the stem ginger.

Serves 4

PORT AND PRUNE FOOL

1 × 439 g (15½ oz) can prunes, drained and stoned
1 × 284 ml (½ pint) carton double cream, whipped
4 tablespoons port
50 g (2 oz) soft brown sugar
grated nutmeg
chopped nuts to decorate

Chop the prunes and fold them into the cream with the port, sugar and nutmeg to taste.

Spoon into individual glass dishes and chill. Decorate with chopped nuts before serving.

Serves 4

MONT BLANC MERINGUES

120 ml (4 fl oz) double cream, whipped
1 × 227 g (8 oz) can sweetened chestnut purée
2 tablespoons Grand Marnier
8 meringue nests
flaked almonds, toasted to decorate

Fold half the cream into the chestnut purée with the Grand Marnier.

Pile the chestnut cream into the meringue nests. Swirl the remaining cream on top to resemble a snow-capped peak. Decorate with almonds. Serve immediately.

Serves 4

ICED CHOCOLATE MINT MERINGUES

25 g (1 oz) plain chocolate, chopped
4 portions soft vanilla ice cream
8 meringue nests
4 tablespoons crème de menthe or Royal mint chocolate liqueur
grated chocolate to decorate (optional)

Fold the chocolate into the ice cream and spoon a portion into each meringue nest. Sprinkle the liqueur over the top. Decorate with grated chocolate, if liked. Serve immediately.

Serves 4

VARIATION: Use chopped peppermint chocolate sticks instead of plain chocolate.

LEFT: *Ginger Log; Port and Prune Fool; Mont Blanc Meringues*
RIGHT: *Iced Chocolate Mint Meringues; Puerto Rican Coffee Ice*

PUERTO RICAN COFFEE ICE

1 × 212 g (7½ oz) can peach slices, drained
4 tablespoons Tia Maria or Grand Marnier
75 g (3 oz) granulated sugar
2 tablespoons water
75 g (3 oz) flaked almonds, toasted
4 portions coffee ice cream

Divide the peach slices between 4 glass dishes, sprinkle with the liqueur and set aside.

Put the sugar and water into a small pan over low heat until dissolved, then boil steadily for 3 to 4 minutes until the syrup turns light brown. Immediately stir in the almonds and pour onto an oiled baking sheet. Leave to cool, then break the praline into pieces.

Place a portion of ice cream in each serving dish and top with the praline. Serve immediately.

Serves 4

YOGURT CHEESECAKE

175 g (6 oz) cream cheese
150 g (5 oz) natural low-fat yogurt
2 drops vanilla essence
2 tablespoons thick honey
2 teaspoons lemon juice
1 × 15–18 cm (6–7 inch) flan case
125 g (4 oz) frozen blackberries, thawed

Beat the cheese and yogurt together until smooth. Add the vanilla essence, honey and lemon juice and beat until thoroughly blended.

Spoon into the flan case and top with the blackberries. Chill before serving.

Serves 4

MOROCCAN ORANGE SALAD

4 large oranges
50 g (2 oz) dates, stoned and chopped
25 g (1 oz) flaked almonds
2 tablespoons caster sugar
juice of 2 lemons
ground cinnamon to decorate

Peel and slice the oranges, discarding the pith. Place in a serving dish with the dates and almonds.

Mix together the sugar and lemon juice and pour over the fruit mixture. Chill for at least 2 hours before serving.

Sprinkle with cinnamon to taste. Serve with cream, if liked.

Serves 4

LEFT: *Yogurt Cheesecake; Moroccan Orange Salad*
RIGHT: *Ginger Rum Trifle; Caledonian Cream*

GINGER RUM TRIFLE

1 × 227 g (8 oz) ginger cake, sliced
6 tablespoons rum
1 × 212 g (7½ oz) can pear quarters, drained with 2 tablespoons juice reserved
300 ml (½ pint) cold thick custard
1 × 142 ml (5 fl oz) double cream
1–2 teaspoons icing sugar
flaked almonds, toasted to decorate

Line a medium soufflé dish or glass bowl with half the ginger cake.

Mix the rum with the reserved pear juice and sprinkle half over the cake. Place the pears on top, cover with the remaining cake and pour over the remaining rum mixture.

Spoon the custard over the cake. Whip the cream with the icing sugar until it forms soft peaks. Spoon over the custard and decorate with almonds.

Serves 4

CALEDONIAN CREAM

3 tablespoons ginger marmalade
250 ml (8 fl oz) double cream
3 tablespoons caster sugar
2 tablespoons whisky
2 tablespoons lemon juice
2 egg whites
soft brown or demerara sugar to decorate

Divide the marmalade between 4 individual glass dishes.

Whip the cream until stiff, then fold in the caster sugar, whisky and lemon juice. Whisk the egg whites until stiff and fold into the cream mixture.

Spoon the cream mixture over the marmalade and sprinkle with brown sugar to decorate.

Serves 4

Exotic Fruit Salad

EXOTIC FRUIT SALAD

2 kiwi fruit, thinly sliced
1 mango, cut into wedges
2 bananas, cut into diagonal slices and tossed in lemon juice
2 guavas, cut into 8 sections, or 2 passion fruit, halved and contents removed with a spoon onto a saucer
½ melon, cut into slices
3 fresh pineapple slices, cut into pieces
2 punnets of raspberries or strawberries
1–2 tablespoons water
caster sugar to taste

Divide the prepared fruit, except the raspberries or strawberries, between 4 individual serving dishes, arranging the fruit attractively in separate piles.

Place the raspberries or strawberries, water and sugar in an electric blender or food processor and work to a purée. Rub through a sieve to remove the pips.

Just before serving, pour some fruit purée into the centre of the fruit; hand any remaining purée separately. Serve with a knife and fork.

Serves 4

MELON WITH STRAWBERRIES

225 g (8 oz) strawberries
4 tablespoons Kirsch or brandy (optional)
2 small ripe Charentais melons, chilled in the refrigerator for at least 6 hours
mint sprigs to decorate

Hull and slice the strawberries. Place in a bowl. Sprinkle the Kirsch or brandy over the strawberries and toss gently. Set aside.

Cut the melons in half and remove the seeds. Scoop out the melon flesh into small balls, using a melon baller or teaspoon. Add to the strawberries and carefully mix the fruits together. Transfer to individual dishes and chill in the refrigerator. Decorate with mint sprigs to serve.

Serves 4

BAKED BANANA PASSION

4 large bananas (or 8 small), sliced lengthways
juice of 2 oranges
2 ripe passion fruit, cut in half
soft light brown sugar to taste (optional)
orange slices to decorate

Grease a shallow ovenproof dish and lay the bananas neatly over the base. Pour over the orange juice and squeeze the passion fruit so that both flesh and pips are used. Sprinkle with sugar to taste, if liked. Bake, uncovered, above the centre of a preheated moderate oven, 180°C (350°F), Gas Mark 4, for 20 minutes. Decorate with orange slices and serve hot.

VARIATION: Use clementines or satsumas instead of oranges, when in season; you will need 3 or 4.

Serves 4

FRUIT WITH WINE AND SPIRITS

A judicious splash of wine or spirits can transform a simple fruit dessert into a special dish. Peaches are particularly delicious with a sweet white wine; strawberries, plums, cherries and melons with a fruity red wine, and oranges with gin. Prepare the fruit just before pouring on the alcohol, sprinkle lightly with sugar, pour on enough alcohol to almost cover the fruit and leave to macerate for an hour or two to let the flavours blend.

MELON AND ORANGE WITH MINT

1 small honeydew melon
2 oranges
few mint leaves, crushed
mint sprigs to decorate

Remove the seeds from the melon, cut the flesh from the skin and chop into pieces. Place in a bowl.

Grate the rind from the orange and add to the melon. Peel and segment the orange, discarding all the pith. Add to the melon with the crushed mint. Mix well and pile into individual serving dishes. Chill.

Decorate with mint sprigs and serve with cream or ice cream.

Serves 4

Melon and Orange with Mint

PEAR AND GINGER CRUMBLE

1 kg (2 lb) ripe cooking pears, peeled, cored and halved
½ teaspoon ground ginger
brown sugar
single cream to serve (optional)

TOPPING:

50 g (2 oz) margarine
25 g (1 oz) butter
175 g (6 oz) wholewheat flour
1 heaped tablespoon wheat bran
2 tablespoons soft brown sugar

Poach the pears in a little water, adding the ginger and sugar to taste, for about 10 to 15 minutes, or until tender.

Meanwhile, make the topping. Rub the margarine and butter into the flour until the mixture resembles coarse breadcrumbs. Stir in the bran and sugar.

Using a slotted spoon, arrange the pears in a greased pie dish. Pour over 2 tablespoons of the cooking liquor and cover with the topping, making a hole in the centre.

Bake above the centre of a preheated moderately hot oven, 200°C (400°F), Gas Mark 6, for about 15 minutes, until browned. Serve hot, with single cream, if desired.

Serves 4 to 6

MANGO-STUFFED APPLES

4 cooking apples, cored
1 mango, chopped
soft light brown sugar to taste
150 ml (5 fl oz) boiling water

Cut a line around the middle of each apple and place in a shallow ovenproof dish. Stuff the core cavities tightly with pieces of mango and sprinkle with sugar. Pour the water into the dish.

Bake in a preheated moderate oven, 180°C (350°F), Gas Mark 4, for 25 to 30 minutes. Serve hot.

Serves 4

VANILLA ICE CREAM

4 eggs, separated
125 g (4 oz) icing sugar, sifted
142 ml (5 fl oz) double cream
142 ml (5 fl oz) single cream
vanilla essence (optional)

Whisk the egg yolks until blended. Whisk the egg whites until they stand in soft peaks, then whisk in the icing sugar a tablespoon at a time until the mixture is stiff.

Whip the creams together until they stand in soft peaks, then fold into the egg white mixture with the yolks. Flavour with vanilla essence, if liked.

Turn into a rigid freezerproof container, cover, seal and freeze until firm.

Leave to stand at room temperature for 5 to 10 minutes before serving or using to soften.

Makes 1.5 litres ($2\frac{1}{2}$ pints)

VARIATIONS:

Strawberry or raspberry: use all double cream, omit the vanilla essence, and proceed as above. Rub 175 g (6 oz) strawberries or raspberries through a sieve, or work in an electric blender or food processor, then sieve to remove pips; there should be 150 ml (5 fl oz) purée. Stir into the ice cream mixture.

Turn into a 1.6 litre ($2\frac{3}{4}$ pint) container and freeze as above.

CHOCOLATE ICE CREAM

1 × 397 g (14 oz) can condensed milk
3 eggs
1 tablespoon cocoa, blended with 2 tablespoons warm water
284 ml (10 fl oz) double cream, whipped

Whisk the condensed milk and eggs together in a heatproof bowl, then stir in the blended cocoa. Place over a pan of simmering water and stir constantly until thick enough to coat the back of the spoon. Remove from the heat and leave to cool. Fold in the cream.

Pour into a rigid freezerproof container, cover, seal and freeze for 1 hour. Stir well, then re-freeze until firm. Use as required.

Makes 1.5 litres ($2\frac{1}{2}$ pints)

Crunchy Strawberry Ice Cream Gâteau (recipe, page 132); Chocolate Nougatine Slice (recipe, page 127); Vanilla, Chocolate and Strawberry Ice Creams

PINEAPPLE FREEZE

1 fresh pineapple
2–4 tablespoons water
125 g (4 oz) icing sugar, sifted
mint sprigs to decorate

Cut the flesh from the pineapple, discarding the central core but leaving the shell intact; reserve the shell. Chop the flesh and place in an electric blender. Add a little water and work to a purée. Stir in the icing sugar.

Pile the mixture into the reserved shell, cover and freeze until firm.

Transfer to the refrigerator 20 minutes before serving to soften slightly. Decorate with mint sprigs.

Serves 4

CHOCOLATE NOUGATINE SLICE

125 g (4 oz) butter
125 g (4 oz) plain chocolate, broken into pieces
125 g (4 oz) digestive biscuits, crushed
50 g (2 oz) blanched almonds, chopped
1 quantity Vanilla Ice Cream (see page 126)

BASE:
150 g (5 oz) flaked almonds
50 g (2 oz) caster sugar

TO DECORATE:
142 ml (5 fl oz) double cream, whipped with 1 tablespoon sifted icing sugar
few flaked almonds, toasted

Place the butter and chocolate in a pan and heat gently until melted. Remove from the heat and stir in the biscuit crumbs and almonds. Turn onto a greased baking sheet and chill until set, then break or chop into pieces.

Soften the ice cream slightly, then stir in the biscuit mixture. Turn into a foil-lined 1 kg (2 lb) loaf tin, cover with foil and put into the freezer while preparing the base.

Place the almonds and sugar in a bowl and mix well. Heat a large frying pan until very hot and tip in the almonds and sugar. Cook over a high heat, stirring constantly, until golden brown and caramelized. Pour onto a lightly greased baking sheet. Leave until set, then crush. Sprinkle over the ice cream and press down firmly. Cover and freeze until firm.

Dip the tin into warm water to loosen the gâteau and turn out onto a chilled serving plate 30 minutes before serving. Decorate with the piped cream and the almonds. Allow to soften slightly in the refrigerator before slicing.

Serves 8

MINT CHOCOLATE CHIP ICE CREAM

3 eggs
75 g (3 oz) caster sugar
300 ml (10 fl oz) milk
284 ml (10 fl oz) double cream, whipped
3 tablespoons crème de menthe
50 g (2 oz) plain chocolate drops

Place the eggs and sugar in a heatproof bowl over a pan of simmering water and whisk until pale and frothy. Heat the milk to just below boiling point and pour onto the eggs. Continue stirring over hot water until thickened. Remove and cool.

Fold the cream into the custard, then stir in the liqueur. Pour into a rigid freezerproof container, cover, seal and freeze for 4 to 5 hours, until there is about 5 cm (2 inches) of solid ice cream around the sides.

Transfer the ice cream to a food processor and work until soft. Add the chocolate drops and process for 5 to 10 seconds. Return to the freezer until firm.

Transfer to the refrigerator 30 to 50 minutes before serving, to soften. Scoop into chilled dishes to serve.

Serves 4–6

Mint Chocolate Chip Ice Cream

ROSE BOMBE

125 g (4 oz) meringues
426 ml (15 fl oz) double cream
1 tablespoon brandy
icing sugar
1 × 425 g (15 oz) can blackberries, drained
1 × 213 g ($7\frac{1}{2}$ oz) can raspberries, drained

TO DECORATE:
142 ml (5 fl oz) double cream, whipped
1 × 213 g ($7\frac{1}{2}$ oz) can raspberries, drained
chocolate leaves

Roughly break up the meringues.

Whip the cream until stiff, add the brandy and icing sugar to taste, then fold in the fruit and meringues. Spoon the mixture into a 1.25 litre ($2\frac{1}{4}$ pint) pudding basin, cover, seal and freeze until firm.

Dip the basin into warm water to loosen the bombe and turn out onto a chilled serving plate 30 minutes before serving. Decorate with piped cream, raspberries and chocolate rose leaves and allow to soften slightly in the refrigerator before slicing.

Serves 8

FESTIVAL BOMBE

150 g (5 oz) mixed crystallized or glacé fruit, chopped
4 tablespoons brandy
3 eggs, separated
75 g (3 oz) caster sugar
284 ml (10 fl oz) double cream, whipped
50 g (2 oz) flaked almonds, toasted

TO DECORATE:
142 ml (5 fl oz) double cream, whipped
75 g (3 oz) glacé cherries, sliced

Place the chopped fruit and brandy in a bowl, cover and leave overnight.

Whisk the egg yolks until frothy. Whisk the egg whites until stiff, then gradually whisk in the sugar.

Fold the cream, egg yolks, almonds, chopped fruit and brandy into the egg whites. Turn into a 1.5 litre ($2\frac{1}{2}$ pint) pudding basin. Cover with foil and freeze until firm.

Dip the basin into warm water to loosen the bombe and turn out onto a chilled serving plate 30 minutes before serving. Cover with stars of piped cream and decorate with glacé cherries. Place in the refrigerator to soften slightly before slicing.

Serves 8

ORANGE CHARLOTTE

2 eggs
100 g ($3\frac{1}{2}$ oz) soft light brown sugar
3 tablespoons water
50 g (2 oz) crystallized orange, chopped, or 1 tablespoon orange marmalade
284 ml (10 fl oz) double cream, whipped
24 sponge fingers
4 tablespoons orange juice
3 tablespoons brandy

TO DECORATE:
142 ml (5 fl oz) double cream, whipped

Whisk the eggs until frothy. Heat the sugar and water until dissolved. Boil, without stirring, for 3 minutes or until syrupy. Pour onto the eggs in a steady stream, whisking constantly until thickened. Stir in the chopped orange or marmalade and leave until cold. Fold the cream into the mixture.

Line the base of a 1.2 litre (2 pint) charlotte mould with greaseproof paper. Arrange 18 of the sponge fingers around the side, trimming to fit neatly. Mix the orange juice and brandy together and brush over the sponge fingers.

Spoon in half the orange mixture and crumble the remaining sponge fingers on top. Drizzle over the remaining orange juice and brandy mixture and cover with the remaining orange cream. Open-freeze until firm.

Turn out onto a chilled serving plate 30 minutes before serving. Decorate with piped cream and allow to soften in the refrigerator.

Serves 8

CHOCOLATE TORTONI

175 g (6 oz) plain chocolate, broken into pieces
142 ml (5 fl oz) single cream
2 tablespoons Kirsch
284 ml (10 fl oz) double cream, whipped
50 g (2 oz) ratafias, finely crushed

TO DECORATE:
40 g ($1\frac{1}{2}$ oz) ratafias
4 tablespoons double cream, whipped
plain chocolate buttons

Place the chocolate and single cream in a small pan and heat gently until melted. Stir well until smooth, then leave until cool. Stir in the Kirsch.

Whisk the Kirsch and chocolate mixture into the whipped cream, then fold in the crushed ratafias. Spoon into a 500 g (1 lb) loaf tin and smooth the surface. Cover with foil, seal and freeze overnight.

Turn upside down over a chilled serving plate and rub the tin with a cloth wrung out in very hot water until the ice cream drops out.

Press the ratafia crumbs over the top and sides of the ice cream. Pipe the cream down the centre and decorate with the chocolate buttons.

Serves 8

Festival Bombe; Rose Bombe; Orange Charlotte

BOMBE AU CHOCOLAT

1 quantity Chocolate Ice Cream (see page 126) or 1.5 litres ($1\frac{1}{4}$ pints) purchased ice cream
142 ml (5 fl oz) double cream
1 tablespoon Kirsch
1 tablespoon icing sugar, sifted
50 g (2 oz) ratafias, halved
chocolate scrolls or curls to decorate

Leave the ice cream at room temperature for 30 minutes to soften. Chill a 1.5 litre ($2\frac{1}{2}$ pint) bombe mould or pudding basin in the refrigerator.

Whip the cream, Kirsch and icing sugar together until stiff peaks form, then fold in the ratafias.

Line the mould or basin thickly with the chocolate ice cream. Fill the centre with the cream and cover with any remaining ice cream. Put on the lid of the bombe mould or cover the basin and foil, seal and freeze overnight.

Dip the mould or basin into cold water to loosen the bombe and turn out onto a chilled serving plate to serve. Decorate with chocolate scrolls or curls.

Serves 6 to 8

VANILLA AND CHOCOLATE RING

$\frac{1}{2}$ quantity Chocolate Ice Cream (see page 126)
$\frac{1}{2}$ quantity Vanilla Ice Cream (see page 126)
TO DECORATE:
142 ml (5 fl oz) double cream, whipped
chocolate triangles

Turn the Chocolate Ice Cream into a 1.25 litre ($2\frac{1}{2}$ pint) ring mould. Cover with foil and freeze for 3 hours.

Spoon the Vanilla Ice Cream on top of the chocolate ice cream, cover with foil, seal and freeze overnight.

Dip the mould in warm water and turn out the ice cream onto a chilled serving plate. Decorate the top with piped cream rosettes and chocolate triangles.

Serves 8

NOTE: If you do not have stocks of homemade ice cream in your freezer, you can make this recipe using 1.25 litres ($1\frac{1}{4}$ pints) each of purchased chocolate and vanilla ice cream.

Bombe au Chocolat; Vanilla and Chocolate Ring

CHOCOLATE MINT ICE

MINT ICE CREAM:
3 egg yolks
150 g (5 oz) caster sugar
284 ml (10 fl oz) single cream
284 ml (10 fl oz) double cream, whipped
3 tablespoons crème de menthe
few drops of green food colouring
TO SERVE:
25 g (1 oz) plain chocolate, melted
1 quantity Bitter Chocolate Sauce (see page 132)

Beat the egg yolks and sugar together until creamy. Bring the single cream to the boil, pour onto the egg yolks and mix thoroughly. Transfer to the top of a double boiler, or a heatproof bowl over a pan of hot water, and cook, stirring constantly, until thick enough to coat the back of the spoon. Strain into a bowl and leave until cool.

Fold into the whipped cream with the crème de menthe and green food colouring, then turn into a 1 kg (2 lb) loaf tin, cover with foil, seal and freeze until firm.

Dip tin into cold water to loosen the ice cream and turn out onto a chilled dish. Place in the refrigerator for about 15 minutes to soften.

Place the warm chocolate in a greaseproof paper piping bag and snip off the end. Cut the ice cream into slices and place on serving plates. Drizzle the chocolate across each slice and serve with the chocolate sauce.

Serves 4–6

NOTE: For a quicker way of making this ice cream, buy 1.5 litres (2½ pints) vanilla ice cream, allow it to soften a little, then beat in the crème de menthe and green food colouring. Freeze until firm.

CHOCOLATE DECORATIONS

Chocolate caraque is made by pouring a thin layer of melted chocolate onto a cold surface and spreading it with a palette knife until it begins to set. When it is hard, take a sharp thin-bladed knife and, holding the handle and tip of the blade, push the knife slightly into the chocolate and scrape in a quarter-circle movement to produce long thin scrolls.

To make chocolate curls, use a vegetable or potato peeler and scrape directly from the block of chocolate. Make sure the chocolate is at room temperature, otherwise the curls will not form properly and will break into pieces.

If you do not have time to make your own decorations, you will find that there is a wide variety in the shops. Among the many are leaves, filigree shapes, vermicelli, dots, candy covered chocolate beans and miniature flakes.

CHOCOLATE BRANDY BOMBES

175 g (6 oz) plain chocolate, broken into pieces
3 tablespoons water
2 eggs, separated
125 g (4 oz) caster sugar
284 ml (10 fl oz) double cream
2 tablespoons brandy
75 g (3 oz) meringues, broken into pieces
TO SERVE:
1 quantity Bitter Chocolate Sauce (see page 132)

Place the chocolate and the water in a small pan and heat gently until the chocolate has melted. Stir in the egg yolks and leave to cool.

Whisk the egg whites until they form stiff peaks, then gradually whisk in the sugar.

Whip the cream and brandy together until soft peaks form, then fold in the chocolate mixture. Carefully fold in the whisked egg whites and broken meringues.

Turn into a 1.5 litre (2½ pint) pudding basin, or into eight 175 ml (6 fl oz) individual moulds, cover with foil, seal and freeze until firm.

Dip each mould into warm water and turn out onto a serving dish. Pour some of the chocolate sauce over the top and serve the rest separately.

Serves 8

Chocolate Brandy Bombes

Coffee Marshmallow Ice Cream Gâteau

CRUNCHY STRAWBERRY ICE CREAM GÂTEAU

750 ml ($1\frac{1}{4}$ pints) chocolate ice cream
1 × 425 g (15 oz) can black cherries, drained and stoned
750 ml ($1\frac{1}{4}$ pints) strawberry ice cream
50 g (2 oz) butter
2 teaspoons golden syrup
50 g (2 oz) plain chocolate, chopped
175 g (6 oz) digestive biscuits, crushed

TO DECORATE:
142 ml (5 fl oz) double cream, whipped

Soften the chocolate cream just enough to fold in the cherries and spoon into a lined and greased 20 cm (8 inch) loose-bottomed cake tin. Cover with foil and freeze until firm.

Soften the strawberry ice cream just enough to spread and spoon over the chocolate layer. Cover, seal and freeze until just firm.

Melt the butter and syrup in a small pan. Add the chocolate and stir until melted, then stir in the biscuit crumbs. Spoon this mixture over the ice cream, press down firmly, cover and freeze until firm.

Dip the tin into warm water to loosen the gâteau and turn out onto a chilled serving plate 30 minutes before serving. Decorate with the whipped cream and allow to soften in the refrigerator before slicing.

Serves 6 to 8

COFFEE MARSHMALLOW ICE CREAM GÂTEAU

125 g (4 oz) puffed wheat cereal
250 g (8 oz) plain chocolate, melted
4 eggs, separated
1 × 397 g (14 oz) can condensed milk
3 teaspoons instant coffee powder
2 teaspoons boiling water
4 teaspoons Tia Maria
284 ml (10 fl oz) double cream
142 ml (5 fl oz) whipping cream
125g (4 oz) marshmallows, chopped
50 g (2 oz) blanched almonds, chopped

Stir the puffed wheat into the chocolate and press over the base and well up the side of a lined and greased 25 cm (10 inch) loose-bottomed cake tin. Chill for 30 minutes.

Blend the egg yolks and condensed milk together. Dissolve the coffee in the water, cool slightly, then stir in the Tia Maria. Beat into the egg yolk mixture.

Whip the creams together until thick, then fold into the custard with the stiffly whisked egg whites, marshmallows and almonds. Pour into the prepared tin and open-freeze until firm.

Dip the tin into warm water to loosen the gâteau and turn out onto a chilled serving plate 30 minutes before serving. Place in the refrigerator to soften slightly before slicing.

Serves 10

CHOCOLATE SAUCES

If you have the time, it is well worth making your own sauces to serve with ice cream, and chocolate sauces are always a particular favourite. For 300 ml ($\frac{1}{2}$ pint) Bitter Chocolate Sauce, break 175 g (6 oz) dark chocolate into pieces and place in a small saucepan with 150 ml ($\frac{1}{4}$ pint) water, 1 teaspoon instant coffee granules and 50 g (2 oz) sugar and heat gently until the sugar has dissolved. Bring to the boil and simmer for 10 minutes, then serve immediately or leave to cool.

For a thicker, creamier texture, try Chocolate and Orange Sauce. To make 450 ml ($\frac{3}{4}$ pint), break 125 g (4 oz) plain chocolate into a small saucepan, add the juice of 1 orange and a 170 g (6 oz) can evaporated milk. Heat gently until the mixture has melted, then bring to the boil and simmer for 3 minutes. Finally, stir in 2 tablespoons of Cointreau. This sauce can be served warm or cold.

COFFEE ICE CREAM

142 ml (5 fl oz) single cream
150 ml ($\frac{1}{4}$ pint) strong coffee made from freshly ground coffee beans
4 egg yolks
125 g (4 oz) caster sugar
284 ml (10 fl oz) double cream
2 tablespoons iced water

Place the single cream and coffee in a pan and warm gently until lukewarm. Remove from the heat and set aside.

Whisk the egg yolks and sugar together until the mixture is pale and thick. Whisk in the coffee cream and return the mixture to the pan. Heat gently, stirring constantly, until the custard thickens. Set aside to cool.

Whip the double cream with the water until it forms soft peaks. Add the coffee custard and beat lightly. Turn into a freezerproof container. Cover, seal and freeze until firm.

Transfer to the refrigerator 30 minutes before serving to soften. Scoop into chilled glasses to serve.

Serves 4

RASPBERRY ICE CREAM SUNDAE

350 g (12 oz) raspberries, fresh or frozen
juice of 1 orange
juice of 1 lemon
175 g (6 oz) granulated sugar
426 ml (15 fl oz) double cream
3 tablespoons iced water
TO SERVE:
175 g (6 oz) raspberries
3 tablespoons Kirsch or brandy
2 tablespoons toasted almonds

Rub the raspberries through a sieve or purée in an electric blender, then sieve to remove pips.

Mix the purée with the orange and lemon juices and the sugar. Chill in the refrigerator for about 1 hour.

Whip the cream with the water until it forms soft peaks. Stir in the raspberry purée and beat lightly together. Turn into a rigid freezer proof container. Cover, seal and freeze for 1 hour. Meanwhile, soak the raspberries in the liqueur.

Remove the ice cream from the freezer; stir, then freeze until solid.

Transfer to the refrigerator 30 minutes before serving to soften. Spoon half the raspberries into 4 chilled glasses and scoop the ice cream on top. Top with the remaining raspberries and almonds.

Serves 4

Coffee Ice Cream; Raspberry Ice Cream Sundae

COFFEE CREAM FINGER BAR

175 g (6 oz) butter
3 egg yolks
4 tablespoons icing sugar, sifted
2 tablespoons strong black coffee, chilled
16 sponge fingers
2 × 284 ml (10 fl oz) cartons double cream, whipped
125 g (4 oz) flaked almonds, toasted
instant coffee powder to decorate

Beat the butter until pale and fluffy, beat in the egg yolks one at a tiime, then beat in the icing sugar. Add the coffee drop by drop, beating until the mixture is thick and creamy.

Arrange 2 horizontal lines of 4 sponge fingers on a serving plate. Spread with half the coffee mixture and a thin layer of cream. Repeat these 2 layers, then top with remaining sponge fingers.

Cover the cake with most of the remaining cream and pipe the rest on top. Press the almonds on the sides.

Spoon some instant coffee powder onto a piece of greaseproof paper. Lay the end of a skewer in the powder, then press it lightly on the surface of the cake to make diagonal lines.

Serves 8

CHOCOLATE ORANGE LAYER

125 g (4 oz) butter
125 g (4 oz) icing sugar, sifted
3 egg yolks
125 g (4 oz) plain chocolate, melted
finely grated rind of 1 orange
2 tablespoons brandy
2 tablespoons orange juice
18–20 sponge fingers
284 ml (10 fl oz) double cream, whipped
3 oranges, segmented

Cream the butter and icing sugar together until light, then beat in the egg yolks a little at a time. Stir in the chocolate and orange rind and set aside.

Mix the brandy and orange juice together in a shallow dish and dip in the sponge fingers. Arrange in a single layer in a greased and lined 500 g (1 lb) loaf tin. Spread with half the chocolate mixture, then spread a thin layer of whipped cream on top, followed by a layer of orange segments, reserving some for decoration, and the remaining chocolate mixture. Top with remaining sponge fingers. Cover and chill for about 1 hour until set.

Turn out onto a serving plate, cover with a thin layer of cream and pipe the rest in swirls around the edge. Decorate with the remaining orange segments.

Serves 8

Coffee Cream Finger Bar; Chocolate Orange Layer

PEAR AND WALNUT CAKE

30 sponge fingers
65g ($2\frac{1}{2}$ oz) butter
125 g (4 oz) icing sugar, sifted
2 egg yolks
$1\frac{1}{2}$ teaspoons instant coffee powder, dissolved in 1 teaspoon hot water
284 ml (10 fl oz) double cream
284 ml (10 fl oz) whipping cream
$1\frac{1}{2}$ teaspoons gelatine, dissolved in 2 tablespoons water
125 g (4 oz) walnuts, thinly sliced
1 × 411 g ($14\frac{1}{2}$ oz) can pear halves, drained and sliced

Arrange a layer of sponge fingers in a lined 23 cm (9 inch) loose-bottomed cake tin.

Cream the butter and icing sugar together, then beat in the egg yolks and coffee.

Whip the creams together until firm and fold into the butter mixture. Add the dissolved gelatine.

Cover the sponge fingers with a third of the cream mixture. Sprinkle lightly with a third of the walnuts and cover with half the sliced pears. Repeat the layers. Cover with the remaining sponge fingers and finish with the remaining cream and a 1 cm ($\frac{1}{2}$ inch) border of walnuts. Chill in the refrigerator until firm.

Carefully remove from the tin and place on a serving plate.

Serves 8

RICH CHOCOLATE BAR WITH BRANDIED FRUIT

125 g (4 oz) raisins
7 tablespoons brandy
75 g (3 oz) plain chocolate, melted
284 ml (10 fl oz) double cream, whipped
1 tablespoon milk
16 sponge fingers
TO FINISH:
284 ml (10 fl oz) double cream, whipped
grated chocolate

Soak the raisins in 5 tablespoons of the brandy for at least 1 hour; drain, reserving any brandy.

Fold the chocolate and raisins into the whipped cream. Mix together the milk and remaining brandy, and pour into a dish. Dip in 8 sponge fingers and arrange horizontally in 2 rows on an oblong plate. Spread with the cream mixture. Dip the remaining sponge fingers in the brandy mixture and place on top. Chill until firm.

Spread a thin layer of whipped cream over the cake and use the rest to pipe swirls around the edge. Fill the centre with grated chocolate.

Serves 8

Pear and Walnut Cake; Rich Chocolate Bar with Brandied Fruit

PINEAPPLE TORTE

250 g (8 oz) coconut biscuits, crushed
65 g ($2\frac{1}{2}$ oz) butter
75 g (3 oz) caster sugar
1 egg
1 × 227 g (8 oz) can pineapple pieces, drained
1 × 439 g ($15\frac{1}{2}$ oz) can crushed pineapple, drained
142 ml (5 fl oz) double cream, whipped

Spread the biscuit crumbs in a 23 cm (9 inch) loose-bottomed flan tin.

Beat the butter and sugar together until light and fluffy, then beat in the egg. Spread carefully over the biscuit base.

Arrange the pineapple pieces around the outer edge. Fill the centre with the crushed pineapple. Chill for at least 1 hour.

Carefully remove from the tin and place on a serving plate. Pipe swirls of cream on top to decorate.

Serves 6 to 8

BRAZILIAN CREAM CAKE

250 g (8 oz) ginger biscuits, crushed
4 large bananas
2 tablespoons lemon juice
65 g ($2\frac{1}{2}$ oz) butter
75 g (3 oz) soft light brown sugar
1 egg
1 tablespoon strong black coffee
284 ml (10 fl oz) double cream, whipped
1 banana, sliced
2 teaspoons lemon juice

Spread half the biscuit crumbs in a 20 cm (8 inch) loose-bottomed cake tin.

Lightly mash the bananas with the lemon juice, using a fork. Beat the butter and sugar together until light and fluffy. Beat in the egg, coffee and bananas and spread lightly and evenly into the tin. Cover with the cream and sprinkle with the remaining biscuit crumbs. Chill for at least 1 hour.

Remove from the tin and place on a serving plate. Toss the banana slices in lemon juice and use to decorate.

Serves 6

HONEY CREAM CRUNCH

125 g (4 oz) butter
100 g ($3\frac{1}{2}$ oz) icing sugar, sifted
2 tablespoons clear honey
1 tablespoon cocoa
1 tablespoon orange juice
250 g (8 oz) digestive biscuits, broken into small pieces
142 ml (5 fl oz) double cream
1 teaspoon clear honey

Cream the butter, icing sugar and honey together. Beat in the cocoa and orange juice. Add the broken biscuits and turn into a well greased 20 cm (8 inch) loose-bottomed flan ring standing on a baking sheet. Spread evenly and press down well. Chill overnight in the refrigerator.

Carefully remove from the tin. Whip the cream and honey together until stiff and pipe over the cake.

Serves 8

Brazilian Cream Cake; Honey Cream Crunch

CHOCOLATE HAZELNUT TORTE

75 g (3 oz) plain chocolate, broken into pieces
3 tablespoons water
50 g (2 oz) butter
50 g (2 oz) soft light brown sugar
1 egg yo
75 g (3
haz
and
3 tabl
16–1
284
d
ch

Place the chocolate and water in a heatproof bowl over a pan of simmering water until melted. Remove from the heat and cool.

Cream the butter and sugar together until light and fluffy. Beat in the egg yolk, chocolate and hazelnuts.

Place the sherry in a shallow dish … half the sponge fingers. … layer in a lined and … tin. … cream on … hazelnut … layer of cream, … sponge fingers … Cover and chill

… serving plate. … the remaining … with the chocolate … chocolate.

WALNUT AND HAZELNUT TORTE

75 g (3 oz) walnuts, finely chopped
50 g (2 oz) hazelnuts, finely chopped
250 ml (8 fl oz) milk
125 g (4 oz) unsalted butter
125 g (4 oz) icing sugar, sifted
2 egg yolks
3 tablespoons medium or sweet sherry
25–30 sponge fingers
TO DECORATE:
284 ml (10 fl oz) double cream, whipped
a few hazelnuts and walnuts

Place the nuts under a hot grill until lightly browned. Place in a mixing bowl. Heat the milk until boiling, pour over the nuts and leave to cool.

Cream the butter and icing sugar together until light and fluffy. Beat in the egg yolks a little at a time, then beat in the nut mixture.

Pour the sherry into a shallow dish. Dip in 2 to 3 sponge fingers at a time and arrange in a single layer in a lined 500 g (1 lb) loaf tin. Spread with half the creamed nut mixture. Repeat the layers, finishing with sponge fingers.

Cover with foil and weight down the top lightly with a small can. Leave in the refrigerator overnight.

Turn out onto a serving plate, cover with most of the cream and decorate with piped cream and nuts.

Serves 6

Chocolate Hazelnut Torte; Walnut and Hazelnut Torte

CARAMEL COCONUT LAYER

1 × 397 g (14 oz) can condensed milk
142 ml (5 fl oz) double cream
142 ml (5 fl oz) single cream
300 g (10 oz) Nice biscuits
TO DECORATE:
142 ml (5 fl oz) double cream, whipped
3 tablespoons desiccated coconut, toasted

Immerse the can of condensed milk in boiling water, cover and boil for 3 hours. Drain off the water and leave to cool completely before opening.

Whip the creams together until standing in soft peaks. Reserve 3 tablespoons of the caramelized condensed milk. Use the remainder to sandwich together the biscuits. Arrange a layer of biscuits in a lined 500 g (1 lb) loaf tin and spread with cream. Repeat the layers until all the ingredients have been used, finishing with a biscuit layer. Cover and chill for at least 4 hours or overnight.

Turn the cake out onto a serving plate. Spread the reserved caramelized milk on top. Coat the sides with two-thirds of the cream and the coconut. Pipe the remaining cream on top.
Serves 8

ORANGE AND GINGER BOMBE

3 eggs, separated
pinch of salt
150 g (5 oz) caster sugar
finely grated rind of 2 small oranges
284 ml (10 fl oz) double cream
142 ml (5 fl oz) single cream
250 g (8 oz) ginger biscuits, crushed
TO DECORATE:
142 ml (5 fl oz) double cream, whipped
sugared orange slices

Whisk the egg yolks, salt, half the sugar and the orange rind together until thick and creamy.

Whisk the egg whites until stiff, then gradually whisk in the rest of the sugar.

Whip the creams together until stiff, then fold into the egg yolk mixture with the egg whites.

Spoon a thin layer into a 1.2 litre (2 pint) pudding basin and cover with a layer of biscuit crumbs..Repeat the layers, finishing with crumbs. Cover, seal and freeze until firm.

Dip the basin into warm water to loosen the bombe and turn out onto a chilled serving plate 30 minutes before serving. Decorate with piped cream and the orange slices. Allow to soften slightly before slicing.
Serves 6 to 8

LEMON GINGER SLICE

10 trifle sponges
100 g (3½ oz) unsalted butter, softened
150 g (5 oz) caster sugar
3 eggs, separated
grated rind and juice of 2 lemons
TO DECORATE:
142 ml (5 fl oz) double cream, whipped
100 g (3½ oz) plain chocolate, grated
50 g (2 oz) crystallized ginger, cut into thin strips

Line the base of a 1 kg (2 lb) loaf tin with greaseproof paper.

Cut each sponge into 3 thin slices and line the base and sides of the tin with about half of them.

Beat the butter and sugar together until light and fluffy, then gradually beat in the egg yolks, lemon rind and juice – the mixture will curdle.

Whisk the egg whites until stiff, then fold into the lemon mixture. Spoon half into the tin and cover with a layer of sliced sponges. Spread with the remaining lemon mixture and top with the remaining sponges. Cover and chill overnight.

Turn out and cover with two thirds of the cream. Press the chocolate on the sides. Pipe the remaining cream on top and add the ginger.
Serves 6 to 8

JAMAICAN CREAM ROLL

1 × 376 g (13¼ oz) can crushed pineapple
284 ml (10 fl oz) double cream, whipped
250 g (8 oz) ginger biscuits
1 tablespoon brandy (optional)
125 g (4 oz) plain chocolate, grated, to decorate

Drain the pineapple well, reserving the juice. Fold half the cream into the pineapple and use to sandwich the biscuits together, pressing them one against another in a roll on a large piece of foil.

Sprinkle with 1 tablespoon of the reserved pineapple juice or the brandy, if liked. Wrap firmly in foil and chill overnight.

Place on a serving plate and cover with the remaining cream. Decorate with diagonal stripes of grated chocolate.
Serves 6

RIGHT: *Caramel Coconut Layer; Lemon Ginger Slice; Jamaican Cream Roll*

Chocolate Orange Cups

CHOCOLATE ORANGE CUPS

250 g (8 oz) plain chocolate, melted
50 g (2 oz) sponge cake, crumbled
3 tablespoons orange juice
1 × 212 g ($7\frac{1}{2}$ oz) can mandarin oranges, drained
TO DECORATE:
284 ml (10 fl oz) double cream, whipped

Using a small spatula, spread the chocolate thickly around the inside of 10 paper cake cases placed in a bun tray. Chill until set, then peel off the paper cases. The cups can be made the day before and chilled until required.

Place the cake crumbs and orange juice in a bowl and mix well. Add the oranges, reserving 10 for decoration. Divide among the cases.

Pipe whipped cream over each and decorate with a mandarin segment.

Makes 10

CRUNCHY CLUSTERS

125 g (4 oz) plain chocolate, broken into pieces
1 tablespoon clear honey
2 tablespoons black coffee
250 g (8 oz) granola or crunchy breakfast cereal
25 g (1 oz) walnuts, chopped

Place the chocolate, honey and coffee in a pan and heat gently until melted. Stir in the cereal and walnuts until thoroughly mixed. Spoon into paper cake cases and leave to set.

Makes 12

CHOCOLATE PALMIERS

1 × 212 g ($7\frac{1}{2}$ oz) packet puff pastry
75g (3 oz) sugar
25 g (1 oz) plain chocolate, grated

Roll out the pastry on a surface sprinkled with half the sugar. Sprinkle the remaining sugar on top of the pastry as you roll it out to a rectangle about 30 × 25 cm (12 × 10 inches); trim the edges. Sprinkle with the chocolate.

Take one shorter edge of the pastry and carefully roll it up to the centre. Roll up the other side to meet it. Moisten the rolls with water where they meet and press together to join. Cut into 1 cm ($\frac{1}{2}$ inch) slices and place well apart on a baking sheet, flattening slightly with the heel of your hand.

Bake in a preheated hot oven, 220°C (425°F), Gas Mark 7, for 10 to 12 minutes; turn them over when they begin to brown so that both sides caramelize. Transfer to a wire rack to cool.

Makes 18 to 20

CHOC-NUT TRUFFLES

250 g (8 oz) sponge cake crumbs
125 g (4 oz) digestive biscuits, crushed
3 tablespoons cocoa powder
50 g (2 oz) hazelnuts, ground and browned
4 tablespoons apricot jam
4 tablespoons chocolate vermicelli

Mix the cake and biscuit crumbs, cocoa and hazelnuts together in a bowl. Add the jam and mix to a stiff paste.

Form the mixture into balls the size of a walnut and roll in the chocolate vermicelli.

Serve the truffles in paper cake cases.

Makes 16 to 18

CHOCOLATE CRUNCHIES

175 g (6 oz) rolled oats
50 g (2 oz) soft light brown sugar
120 ml (4 fl oz) corn oil
1 egg
125 g (4 oz) plain chocolate, melted

Place the oats, sugar, oil and egg in a bowl and beat together thoroughly. Place teaspoonfuls of the mixture well apart on a greased baking sheet and flatten with a dampened fork.

Bake in a preheated moderate oven, 160°C (325°F), Gas Mark 3, for 15 to 20 minutes, until golden brown. Leave to cool for 1 minute, then transfer to a wire rack to cool completely.

Spread the chocolate over the flat underside of each biscuit. Place chocolate side up on a wire rack, leave to set slightly, then mark into lines with a palette knife. Leave until set.

Makes 20

BRAN CRUNCH

50 g (2 oz) butter
2 tablespoons clear honey
125 g (4 oz) plain chocolate, broken into pieces
75 g (3 oz) bran flakes
25 g (1 oz) walnuts, chopped

Place the butter, honey and chocolate in a pan and heat gently, stirring, until melted. Add the bran flakes and walnuts and mix thoroughly.

Turn into a lined and greased shallow 18 cm (7 inch) square cake tin, smooth the surface and chill until set. Cut into triangles to serve.

Makes 8

CHOC-NUT CURLS

75 g (3 oz) butter or margarine
75 g (3 oz) caster sugar
40 g (1½ oz) plain flour, sifted
15 g (½ oz) cocoa powder, sifted
50 g (2 oz) hazelnuts, chopped

Cream the butter or margine and sugar together until light and fluffy. Stir in the flour, cocoa and hazelnuts and mix well. Place teaspoonfuls of the mixture well apart on greased baking sheets (see note) and flatten with a dampened fork.

Bake in a preheated moderately hot oven, 200°C (400°F), Gas Mark 6, for 6 to 8 minutes, until pale golden.

Leave on the baking sheets for 1 minute then remove with a palette knife and place on a rolling pin to curl. Leave until set then remove very carefully.

Makes 20 to 24

NOTE: Do not bake more than 4 at a time or they will set before you have time to shape them.

Chocolate Crunchies; Bran Crunch

TREACLE TARTLETS

1 × 175 g (6 oz) packet shortcrust pastry tray, thawed if frozen
250 g (8 oz) golden syrup
50 g (2 oz) fresh white breadcrumbs
2 teaspoons lemon juice

Roll out pastry on a floured surface and use to line a 12-hole deep bun tray.

Place the syrup in a pan and heat gently until melted, then stir in the breadcrumbs and lemon juice. Divide among the pastry cases and decorate with pastry trimmings.

Bake in a preheated hot oven, 200°C (400°F), Gas Mark 6, for 10 to 15 minutes. Serve warm or cold.

Makes 12

FLORENTINES

75 g (3 oz) flaked almonds
50 g (2 oz) cut mixed peel
50 g (2 oz) glacé cherries, quartered
50 g (2 oz) butter, melted
50 g (2 oz) caster sugar
1 tablespoon double cream
125 g (4 oz) plain chocolate, melted

Mix the almonds, peel and cherries together. Stir into the butter, together with the sugar and cream. Leave until cold. Place teaspoonfuls of the mixture well apart on greased and floured baking sheets.

Bake in a preheated moderately hot oven, 190°C (375°F), Gas Mark 5, for about 8 minutes until pale golden brown round the edge. Reshape, using a large pastry cutter, and leave on the baking sheet until almost cold. Transfer to a wire rack, flat sides up, and spread thinly with the melted chocolate.

Makes about 30

Florentines

LEMON VIENNESE TARTS

250 g (8 oz) butter, softened
75 g (3 oz) icing sugar
175 g (6 oz) plain flour
50 g (2 oz) cornflour
1 teaspoon finely grated lemon rind
TO DECORATE:
2 tablespoons icing sugar
2 tablespoons lemon curd

Place the butter, icing sugar, flour, cornflour and lemon rind in a food processor and work until soft and thoroughly blended.

Put the mixture into a piping bag fitted with a 2.5 cm (1 inch) fluted nozzle and pipe into 12 paper cases, placed in a bun tray, using a circular movement.

Bake in a preheated moderate oven, 180°C (350°F), Gas Mark 4, for 20 minutes, until pale in colour. Transfer to a wire rack to cool.

Sift with icing sugar and put a little lemon curd in the centre of each tart.

Makes 12

FRESH FRUIT TARTLETS

75 g (3 oz) margarine, cut into small pieces
175 g (6 oz) wholewheat flour
2 tablespoons ground almonds
4 drops almond essence
2 teaspoons soft brown sugar
2–3 tablespoons water
TOPPING:
1 × 142 ml (5 fl oz) carton double cream
1 teaspoon caster sugar
prepared fresh fruit: kiwi fruit, strawberries, raspberries, pineapple, mango, lychees, etc.
caster sugar (optional)

Put the margarine, flour, ground almonds and almond essence into a bowl and rub in until the mixture resembles breadcrumbs. Stir in the sugar and enough water to make a moist dough. Sprinkle in a little more flour and knead lightly.

Roll out the pastry on a floured surface, cut into rounds with a 6 cm ($2\frac{1}{2}$ inch) fluted cutter and use to line 12 bun tins. Bake on the top shelf of a preheated hot oven, 230°C (450°F), Gas Mark 8, for 10 minutes. Cool on a wire rack.

Whip the cream with the sugar and put a heaped teaspoon into each pastry case. Top with fruit and sprinkle with a little sugar, if liked.

Makes 12

Treacle Tart; Orange Tart

TREACLE TART

1 × 212 g ($7\frac{1}{2}$ oz) packet shortcrust pastry, thawed if frozen
4 tablespoons cornflakes, crushed, or fresh white breadcrumbs
6 tablespoons golden syrup, warmed
juice of $\frac{1}{2}$ lemon
$\frac{1}{2}$ teaspoon ground ginger

Roll out the pastry and use to line a 20 cm (8 inch) ovenproof plate. Trim, knock up the edge and flute. Reserve the pastry trimmings. Prick the pastry base.

Sprinkle half the cornflakes or breadcrumbs in the pastry case and pour in the syrup. Sprinkle the lemon juice over the syrup.

Mix the ginger with the remaining cornflakes or breadcrumbs and sprinkle over the top. Cut strips from the pastry trimmings and make a lattice pattern over the tart.

Cook in a preheated moderately hot oven, 190°C (375°F), Gas Mark 5 for 30 minutes until the pastry is crisp and golden. Serve hot or cold with whipped cream or ice cream.

Serves 4

ORANGE TART

1 × 212 g ($7\frac{1}{2}$ oz) packet shortcrust pastry, thawed if frozen
2 oranges, thinly sliced
1 egg, beaten
50 g (2 oz) ground almonds
1 tablespoon sugar
2 tablespoons clear honey

Roll out the pastry and use to line a 20 cm (8 inch) flan dish. Prick the base. Line with a piece of greaseproof paper and dried beans. Bake blind in a preheated moderately hot oven, 190°C (375°F), Gas Mark 5, for 15 minutes. Remove the beans and paper.

Meanwhile, put the oranges in a small pan. Add just enough water to cover and simmer for about 30 minutes until the peel is tender. Drain.

Beat together the egg, almonds and sugar until smooth. Spread in the flan case and arrange the orange slices on top. Spoon over the honey. Return to the oven for 20 minutes.

Serve hot or cold, with cream.

Serves 4

SPONGE DROPS

3 eggs
125 g (4 oz) caster sugar
125 g (4 oz) plain flour, sifted
TO FINISH:
25 g (1 oz) caster sugar
2 tablespoons raspberry jam
284 ml (10 fl oz) double cream, whipped

Whisk the eggs and sugar together until pale and thick. Gently fold in the flour.

Place the mixture in a piping bag fitted with a 1 cm (½ inch) plain nozzle. Pipe into discs, 3.5 cm (1½ inches) in diameter, on lined baking sheets, 5 cm (2 inches) apart; there should be enough for about 48 discs. Sift a little sugar over them and bake in a preheated moderately hot oven, 190°C (375°F), Gas Mark 5, for 10 minutes or until light golden brown. Cool on the baking sheets.

When cold, dampen the underside of the lining paper and carefully peel off the discs. Sandwich together in pairs with jam and cream.

Makes about 24

NOTE: This very light mixture quickly loses its volume if handled heavily or left to stand, so speed and gentleness are essential. Make sure you have all the ingredients at room temperature before you start.

WALNUT MERINGUES

2 egg whites
125 g (4 oz) icing sugar, sifted
50 g (2 oz) walnuts, finely chopped

Whisk the egg whites until stiff. Add the icing sugar a tablespoon at a time and whisk until very thick. Carefully fold in the walnuts. Place small mounds of the mixture on a baking sheet lined with non-stick paper.

Bake in a preheated moderate oven, 180°C (350°F), Gas Mark 4, for 15 to 20 minutes. Leave to cool slightly, then carefully transfer to a wire rack to cool completely.

Makes 22

OATMEAL CRUNCHIES

250 g (8 oz) self-raising flour, sifted
50 g (2 oz) porridge oats
75 g (3 oz) granulated sugar
75 g (3 oz) soft light brown sugar
¼ teaspoon salt
125 g (4 oz) butter
3 teaspoons golden syrup
2 tablespoons milk

Put the flour, oats, sugars and salt into a bowl and mix well. Rub in the butter to form a crumble consistency. Mix the syrup and milk together, add to the dry ingredients and mix to a stiff dough. Knead lightly and shape into a roll, 5 cm (2 inches) in diameter. Chill for about 1 hour until very firm, then cut into 5 mm (¼ inch) thick slices. Place on greased baking sheets, 1 cm (½ inch) apart.

Bake in a preheated moderately hot oven, 190°C (375°F), Gas Mark 5, for 15 minutes. Leave on the baking sheet for 1 minute, then transfer to a wire rack to cool.

Makes 30

FLAPJACKS

175 g (6 oz) butter
25 g (1 oz) golden syrup
125 g (4 oz) soft light brown sugar
250 g (8 oz) porridge oats
50 g (2 oz) desiccated coconut

Melt the butter and syrup together in a pan. Remove from the heat and stir in the remaining ingredients. Turn into a greased 18 × 28 cm (7 × 11 inch) Swiss roll tin and spread evenly.

Bake in a preheated moderate oven, 180°C (350°F), Gas Mark 4, for 15 minutes. Cool slightly, then cut into fingers and remove from the tin.

Makes 22

ABOVE: *Blackberry Crunch*
LEFT: *Sponge Drops*

BLACKBERRY CRUNCH

50 g (2 oz) butter
2 tablespoons golden syrup
200 g (7 oz) digestive biscuits, finely crushed
2 cooking apples, peeled, cored and thinly sliced
1 tablespoon lemon juice
125 g (4 oz) caster sugar
250 g (8 oz) blackberries
2 tablespoons water
2 teaspoons powdered gelatine
1 egg white

Melt the butter and syrup together in a pan, stir in the biscuit crumbs and spread over the base and up the side of a 20 cm (8 inch) fluted flan tin.

Cook the apples in the lemon juice for about 8 minutes or until tender. Beat in half the sugar and leave until cold.

Cook the blackberries in the water and remaining sugar for 2 minutes, until tender. Strain the hot syrup into a bowl, sprinkle on the gelatine and leave until dissolved, stirring if necessary. Chill until almost set.

Spread the apple purée over the biscuit base and top with the blackberries.

Whisk the egg white until stiff, then whisk in the blackberry jelly until frothy. Pour on top of the blackberries and chill until set. Serve immediately.

Serves 6

BLACKCURRANT CREAM FLANS

75 g (3 oz) butter
3 tablespoons golden syrup
200 g (7 oz) Rich Tea biscuits, finely crushed
250 g (8 oz) blackcurrants
150 ml ($\frac{1}{4}$ pint) water
125 g (4 oz) sugar
2 tablespoons cornflour
TO DECORATE:
1 × 142 ml (5 fl oz) carton half cream
blackcurrants

Put the butter and syrup into a pan and heat gently until melted. Stir in the biscuit crumbs. Divide the mixture between six 10 cm (4 inch) individual fluted flan tins, pressing firmly over the bases and up the sides.

Put the blackcurrants and water into a saucepan, bring to the boil, then cover and simmer for 5 minutes. Transfer to an electric blender or food processor and work until smooth, then sieve. Make the purée up to 300 ml ($\frac{1}{2}$ pint) with water.

Put the blackcurrant purée, sugar and cornflour into a pan and stir well. Bring to the boil, then cook gently for 1 minute. Fill the biscuit cases with the blackcurrant mixture and leave until cold. Remove from the tins.

Whip the cream until just beginning to thicken, then pour over the flans. Decorate with a few whole blackcurrants.

Serves 6

BISCUITS AND THE MICROWAVE

Most traditional biscuit recipes can be cooked in the microwave. Make up the mixture in the usual way, then arrange 6 biscuits at a time in a ring on a plate or directly on the turntable and cook on HIGH for about $1\frac{1}{2}$–2 minutes. Leave to stand for 2 minutes to crispen, then transfer to a wire rack. For specific instructions, check with your manufacturer's handbook.

Most biscuits will freeze successfully. Open freeze until firm, then pack into a rigid container for up to 4 months.

Depending on type, thaw biscuits at room temperature for about 1–2 hours. Alternatively, arrange about 250 g (8 oz) biscuits around the edge of a plate and cook in the microwave on DEFROST or LOW for 1–$1\frac{1}{2}$ minutes, turning over once. Leave to stand for 5 minutes before serving.

HAZELNUT ROULADE

3 eggs
65 g ($2\frac{1}{2}$ oz) caster sugar
15 g ($\frac{1}{2}$ oz) plain flour
50 g (2 oz) ground hazelnuts
1 × 142 ml (5 fl oz) carton double cream, whipped

TO FINISH:
caster sugar for sprinkling
sifted icing sugar

Whisk the eggs and sugar together until the whisk leaves a trail. Sift the flour onto the mixture, add the nuts and carefully fold together. Turn into a lined and greased 20 × 30 cm (8 × 12 inch) Swiss roll tin. Bake in a preheated moderately hot oven, 200°C (400°F), Gas Mark 6, for 10 to 12 minutes or until springy to touch.

Turn out onto lightly sugared, greaseproof paper placed on a damp, clean tea-towel. Remove the lining paper and trim the edges, if necessary. Carefully roll up the sponge from the short edge with the sugared paper inside and leave until cold. Unroll the sponge and remove the paper. Spread with the cream, then roll up again. Chill until required and sprinkle liberally with icing sugar to serve.
Serves 8

Hazelnut Roulade

SWISS ROLL

3 eggs
125 g (4 oz) caster sugar
75 g (3 oz) plain flour, sifted
1 tablespoon hot water
3 tablespoons warmed jam
caster sugar for dredging

Whisk the eggs and sugar together in a mixing bowl over a pan of hot water until thick enough to leave a trail when the whisk is lifted. (Hot water is unnecessary if you are using an electric beater.) Fold in the flour and water, then turn into a lined and greased 18 × 28 cm (7 × 11 inch) Swiss roll tin and spread out evenly.

Bake in a preheated moderately hot oven, 200°C (400°F), Gas Mark 6, for 8 to 10 minutes until the cake springs back when lightly pressed.

Turn onto sugared greaseproof paper, peel off the lining paper and trim the edges. Cut two-thirds of the way through the short edge nearest you, then spread lightly with the jam and roll up quickly. Hold in position for a few minutes, then transfer to a wire rack to cool. Dredge with caster sugar before serving.
Makes one Swiss roll

BANANA ROULADE

40 g ($1\frac{1}{2}$ oz) self-raising flour
15 g ($\frac{1}{2}$ oz) cocoa powder
3 eggs
50 g (2 oz) caster sugar

FILLING:
3 tablespoons rum
142 ml (5 fl oz) whipping cream, whipped
1 banana

TO DECORATE:
little lemon juice
icing sugar, sifted

Sift the flour and cocoa together twice. Whisk the eggs and sugar together until the whisk leaves a trail. Fold in the flour and cocoa.

Turn into a lined and greased 18 × 28 cm (7 × 11 inch) Swiss roll tin and smooth the surface. Bake in a preheated moderately hot oven, 200°C (400°F), Gas Mark 6, for 12 to 14 minutes or until springy to touch.

Turn out onto lightly sugared greaseproof paper on a damp cloth and remove the lining paper. Using the cloth to help, roll up the sponge from the short edge with the sugared paper inside and leave to cool.

Unroll the sponge, remove the paper and sprinkle with the rum. Spread with the cream, then lay the banana across the roll, a little in from the edge. Roll up the sponge. Trim the ends and brush the ends of the banana with lemon juice. Dust with icing sugar. Chill for 1 hour.
Makes one roulade

CRUNCHY RHUBARB FLANS

50 g (2 oz) butter, melted
200 g (7 oz) coconut biscuits, finely crushed
300 g (10 oz) rhubarb, cut into 2.5 cm (1 inch) lengths
2 tablespoons orange juice
75 g (3 oz) caster sugar
2 tablespoons cornflour
1 egg, separated
4 orange slices to decorate

Combine the butter and biscuit crumbs and divide the mixture between four 10 cm (4 inch) individual flan dishes, pressing over the bases and up the sides.

Put the rhubarb, orange juice and sugar into a saucepan, bring to the boil, then cover and simmer for 4 minutes, or until tender. Work in an electric blender or food processor until smooth, or rub through a sieve.

Put the cornflour into a saucepan and stir in a little rhubarb purée. Add the remaining purée and the egg yolk, bring to the boil, stirring, then simmer for 1 minute.

Whisk the egg white until stiff, then fold into the rhubarb mixture and spoon into the biscuit cases.

Bake in a preheated moderately hot oven, 200°C (400°F), Gas Mark 6, for 8 to 10 minutes, until set.

Serve hot or cold, decorated with a twist of orange.

NOTE: This quantity will also make one 20 cm (8 inch) flan.

Serves 4

SWISS RHUBARB CHEESECAKE

350 g (12 oz) rhubarb, cut into 2.5 cm (1 inch) lengths
2 tablespoons water
50 g (2 oz) caster sugar
15 g ($\frac{1}{2}$ oz) gelatine
227 g (8 oz) curd cheese
142 ml (5 fl oz) soured cream
1 chocolate Swiss roll, thinly sliced
TO DECORATE:
chocolate curls
shredded orange rind
whipped cream

Place the rhubarb and water in a saucepan, bring to the boil, cover and simmer for 4 minutes or until tender. Pour into an electric blender or food processor, sprinkle the sugar and gelatine on top, and work until smooth.

Add the cheese and cream and blend on minimum speed until evenly blended. Pour into a bowl and leave until almost set.

Line the side of a greased 18 cm (7 inch) straight-sided dish or cake tin with Swiss roll slices. Pour the rhubarb mixture into the dish and cover with the remaining Swiss roll slices. Leave to set.

Dip the dish into hot water, then invert onto a serving plate. Decorate with chocolate curls, orange rind and piped cream.

Makes one cheesecake

Crunchy Rhubarb Flans; Swiss Rhubarb Cheesecake

TOFFEE MELBA FLAN

125 g (4 oz) creamy toffees
2 tablespoons water
50 g (2 oz) hazelnuts, toasted and finely chopped
50 g (2 oz) Rice Pops
2 teaspoons powdered gelatine
1 tablespoon water
350 g (12 oz) raspberries
2 tablespoons icing sugar
5 peaches, peeled, stoned and sliced
TO DECORATE:
whipped cream
hazelnuts

Heat the toffees and water gently in a saucepan until melted, stirring occasionally. Stir in the nuts and Rice Pops until well mixed, then press over the base and up the side of a 23 cm (9 inch) fluted flan dish.

Put the gelatine into a cup with the water and leave to soak. Warm gently to dissolve. Rub the raspberries through a sieve into a bowl. Add the dissolved gelatine and icing sugar to the purée and stir until well blended. Leave until almost set, then pour into the lined case and chill until set.

Arrange the peach slices on top and decorate with piped cream and hazelnuts.

Serves 6

ABOVE: *Toffee Melba Flan; Peach Melba Cheesecake*
RIGHT: *Lemon Layer Cheesecake; St Clement's Whip Flan*

PEACH MELBA CHEESECAKE

125 g (4 oz) creamy toffees
2 tablespoons water
200 g (7 oz) chocolate digestive biscuits, crushed
125 g (4 oz) unsalted butter
1 packet peach jelly
5 peaches, peeled and stoned
1 × 227 g (8 oz) carton cottage cheese
1 × 142 ml (5 fl oz) carton single cream
125 g (4 oz) raspberries
50 g (2 oz) sugar
whipped cream to decorate

Heat the toffees and water gently in a pan until melted, stirring occasionally. Stir in the biscuit crumbs, then press over the base of a 20 cm (8 inch) loose-based cake tin.

Put the butter and jelly into a saucepan and heat gently, stirring occasionally, until melted. Place 2 of the peaches in an electric blender or food processor, add the jelly mixture, cheese and cream and work until well blended. Pour into the tin and chill until set.

Sieve the raspberries into a pan, add the sugar and heat gently until dissolved. Boil for 1 minute until syrupy; leave to cool.

Place the cheesecake on a plate and decorate with the remaining peaches, thinly sliced. Brush with the raspberry glaze and decorate with piped cream swirls.

Serves 8

LEMON LAYER CHEESECAKE

125 g (4 oz) margarine
4 tablespoons golden syrup
2 tablespoons cocoa powder
350 g (12 oz) digestive biscuits, finely crushed
15 g (½ oz) powdered gelatine
3 tablespoons water
350 g (12 oz) cream cheese
2 eggs, separated
50 g (2 oz) caster sugar
grated rind and juice of 1 lemon
1 × 142 ml (5 fl oz) carton double cream, whipped
TO DECORATE:
lemon twists
whipped cream

Put the margarine, syrup and cocoa into a saucepan and heat gently until melted, stirring occasionally. Stir in the biscuit crumbs. Spread half the mixture over the base of a 20 cm (8 inch) loose-based cake tin.

Put the gelatine into a cup with the water and leave to soak. Warm gently to dissolve. Beat the cheese, egg yolks and sugar together until smooth, then stir in the lemon rind and juice. Beat in the dissolved gelatine. Whisk the egg whites until stiff, then fold into the lemon mixture with the cream.

Pour half the mixture into the tin and chill until almost set. Cover with the remaining biscuit mixture and top with the remaining lemon mixture. Chill until set.

Carefully remove from the tin and place on a serving plate. Decorate with lemon twists and piped cream.

Serves 8 to 10

ST CLEMENT'S WHIP FLAN

50 g (2 oz) self-raising flour
¼ teaspoon baking powder
2 teaspoons cocoa powder
50 g (2 oz) caster sugar
50 g (2 oz) soft margarine
1 egg
FILLING:
2 teaspoons powdered gelatine
1 tablespoon water
2 eggs, separated
50 g (2 oz) caster sugar
grated rind and juice of 1 small lemon
grated rind of 1 small orange
TO DECORATE:
orange segments
whipped cream

Sift the flour, baking powder and cocoa into a bowl. Add the sugar, margarine and egg and beat for 1 to 2 minutes, until smooth. Spoon into a base-lined and greased 20 cm (8 inch) fluted sponge flan tin and bake in a preheated moderate oven, 160°C (325°F), Gas Mark 3, for 15 to 20 minutes, until firm to touch. Cool on a wire rack while making the filling.

Put the gelatine into a cup with the water and leave to soak. Warm gently to dissolve. Put the egg yolks and sugar into a bowl over a pan of hot water and whisk until thick and creamy. Remove from the heat and stir in the lemon juice and orange and lemon rinds. Stir in the dissolved gelatine and leave until just set.

Whisk the egg whites until stiff, then whisk into the gelatine mixture. Pour into the flan case and decorate with orange segments and piped cream.

Serves 6

LEMON GINGER FLAN

50 g (2 oz) butter, melted
200 g (7 oz) ginger biscuits, finely crushed
1 × 410 g (14½ oz) can condensed milk
grated rind and juice of 2 lemons
1 × 284 ml (½ pint) carton double cream, whipped
TO DECORATE:
50 g (2 oz) preserved ginger, sliced
whipped cream

Combine the butter, biscuit crumbs and 2 tablespoons of the condensed milk. Press the mixture over the base and up the side of a 20 cm (8 inch) plain flan ring placed on a flat plate.

Pour the remaining condensed milk into a bowl, add the lemon rind and juice and beat well. Leave for a few minutes to thicken, then fold in the cream. Pour into the flan case and form into swirls with a palette knife. Leave until set, then remove the flan ring.

Decorate with ginger slices and piped cream.

Serves 6

TANGY CHEESECAKE

50 g (2 oz) butter, melted
200 g (7 oz) ginger biscuits, finely crushed
1 × 410 g (14½ oz) can condensed milk
1 × 227 g (8 oz) packet creamery soft cheese
grated rind and juice of 1 lime
grated rind and juice of 1 lemon
TO DECORATE:
1 × 142 ml (5 fl oz) carton double cream, whipped
lemon and lime rind, cut into petal, leaf and stem shapes

Combine the butter, biscuit crumbs and 2 tablespoons of the condensed milk. Press the mixture over the base of a 20 cm (8 inch) loose-based cake tin.

Beat the cheese in a bowl until softened, then gradually beat in the remaining condensed milk, lime and lemon rind and juice. Leave until the mixture thickens, then fold in the cream. Pour into the tin. Place in the refrigerator until set.

Carefully transfer the cheesecake to a serving plate and decorate with piped cream and flowers made from lime and lemon rind shapes.

Serves 6 to 8

BRAZILIAN CHEESECAKE

8 trifle sponges, halved horizontally
3 tablespoons pineapple juice
1 × 227 g (8 oz) carton cream cheese
1 × 113 g (4 oz) carton cottage cheese, sieved
75 g (3 oz) caster sugar
50 g (2 oz) plain chocolate drops
1 small pineapple, quartered and sliced
TO FINISH:
1 × 142 ml (5 fl oz) carton double cream
1 tablespoon strong coffee
25 g (1 oz) chocolate drops

Line the base and sides of a 1.2 litre (2 lb) loaf tin with foil. Use the sponges to line the base and sides of the tin, reserving 4 pieces for the top. Sprinkle with the pineapple juice.

Beat the cheeses and sugar together, then stir in chocolate drops and two-thirds of the pineapple pieces. Spoon the mixture into the tin and cover with the remaining sponges. Cover with foil and chill for several hours or overnight. Turn out onto a serving plate.

Whip the cream and coffee together until thick and spread a thin layer over the cheesecake. Place the rest in a piping bag fitted with a small star nozzle and pipe whirls around the top of the cheesecake. Decorate with the chocolate drops and arrange the remaining pineapple on top.
Serves 6

FREEZING AND THAWING CHEESECAKES

Cheesecakes are irrestible desserts, so it is well worth making them in bulk for the freezer. For best results open freeze until firm, then overwrap in double thickness polythene or place in a rigid container. Most cheesecakes can be frozen for up to 3 months.

To thaw, remove all wrappings, place the cheesecake on a serving plate and leave in the refrigerator overnight or at room temperature for 4–6 hours. If you are in a hurry, place the cheesecake on a non-metallic plate and cook in the microwave on DEFROST or LOW for 1½–2 minutes, checking frequently to ensure that there is no visible melting. Leave to stand for 15–20 minutes to thaw completely. Cook individual cheesecakes for just 30 seconds and leave to stand for about 10 minutes before serving.

LEFT: *Lemon Ginger Flan; Tangy Cheesecake*
RIGHT: *Summer Lime Cheesecake*

SUMMER LIME CHEESECAKE

8 trifle sponges, halved horizontally
4 tablespoons lime juice or sherry
15 g (½ oz) powdered gelatine
3 tablespoons water
175 g (6 oz) cream cheese
175 g (6 oz) caster sugar
2 eggs, separated
1 × 142 ml (5 fl oz) carton double cream
grated rind and juice of 2 limes
TO DECORATE:
whipping cream, whipped
1 tablespoon plain chocolate drops
1 lime, cut into 10 wedges

Use the sponges to line the base of a 20 cm (8 inch) loose-based cake tin. Sprinkle with the lime juice or sherry.

Put the gelatine into a cup with the water and leave to soak. Warm gently to dissolve. Beat together the cheese and sugar until well blended, then whisk in the egg yolks, cream, lime rind and juice, and dissolved gelatine.

Whisk the egg whites until stiff, carefully fold into the lime mixture until smooth, then pour into the cake tin. Chill until set.

Carefully transfer the cheesecake to a serving plate. Pipe swirls of cream around the top edge and decorate with the chocolate drops. Arrange the lime wedges in the centre.
Serves 8

Chocolate Cheese Cups; Strawberry Crunch

STRAWBERRY CRUNCH

125 g (4 oz) plain chocolate, broken into pieces
25 g (1 oz) butter
2 tablespoons golden syrup
75 g (3 oz) cornflakes, crushed
350 g (12 oz) strawberries
25 g (1 oz) caster sugar
2 teaspoons powdered gelatine
2 tablespoons water
1 × 284 ml (½ pint) carton double cream, whipped
TO DECORATE:
whipped cream
strawberry slices

Melt the chocolate, butter and syrup gently in a saucepan, stirring occasionally. Stir in the cornflakes and press the mixture over the base and up the side of a 23 cm (9 inch) fluted flan dish.

Put the strawberries into an electric blender or food processor and work to a purée. Strain through a sieve to remove pips, if necessary, then stir the sugar into the purée.

Put the gelatine into a cup with the water and leave to soak. Warm gently to dissolve. Stir the dissolved gelatine into the strawberry purée. Fold the purée into the cream, then pour into the flan case. Chill until set.

Decorate with piped cream and strawberry slices.

Serves 6 to 8

CHOCOLATE CHEESE CUPS

175 g (6 oz) plain chocolate, melted
1 ogen melon, halved and seeds removed
125 g (4 oz) strawberries, sliced
1 × 227 g (8 oz) packet creamery soft cheese
4 tablespoons natural low-fat yogurt
25 g (1 oz) caster sugar

Place 10 paper cake cases in bun tins. Divide the melted chocolate between them, brushing over the bases and up the sides to coat evenly. Place in a cool place or refrigerator until set hard.

Carefully peel off each paper case and place the chocolate cups on a serving plate.

Cut out 10 melon balls, using a cutter, and reserve for decoration. Chop the remaining melon.

Reserve 20 strawberry slices for decoration. Divide the rest between the chocolate cups. Cover with chopped melon.

Beat together the creamery soft cheese, yogurt and sugar until smooth. Place in a piping bag fitted with a medium star nozzle and pipe a large swirl on top of the fruit. Decorate each cup with 2 strawberry slices and a melon ball.

Makes 10

MOCHA LAYER CHEESECAKE

350 g (12 oz) skimmed milk soft cheese
1 × 150 g (5 oz) carton natural low-fat yogurt
2 tablespoons caster sugar
50 g (2 oz) plain chocolate, melted
2 teaspoons instant coffee granules
1 teaspoon boiling water
2 packets sponge fingers
2 tablespoons sherry
TO DECORATE:
1 × 284 ml (½ pint) carton whipping cream, whipped

Beat together the cheese, yogurt and half the sugar. Put half the mixture into a separate bowl and beat in the melted chocolate. Blend together the remaining sugar, coffee granules and water and beat into the other mixture.

Dip the sponge fingers in the sherry and use one-third to cover the base of a 1.2 litre (2 lb) loaf tin lined with cling film.

Spread with the chocolate mixture, then cover with sponge fingers.

Cover with the coffee mixture and top with the remaining sponge fingers. Cover and chill.

Invert the cheesecake onto a serving plate. Spread the top and sides with whipped cream and pipe swirls of cream around the top and base.

Serves 6 to 8

MALLOW RASPBERRY FLAN

50 g (2 oz) butter
125 g (4 oz) marshmallows
200 g (7 oz) shortcake biscuits, finely crushed
125 g (4 oz) muesli
1 packet raspberry jelly
150 ml (¼ pint) boiling water
250 g (8 oz) raspberries
1 × 150 g (5 oz) carton raspberry yogurt
TO DECORATE:
whipped cream
raspberries

Put the butter and marshmallows into a bowl over a pan of simmering water until melted, stirring occasionally. Remove from the pan, add the biscuit crumbs and muesli and stir well.

Using a wet metal spoon, press the mixture over the base and up the side of a 25 cm (10 inch) plain flan ring on a flat serving plate. Chill until set.

Dissolve the jelly in the water. Put the raspberries into an electric blender or food processor and work to a purée; sieve. Pour into a measuring jug with the jelly and make up to 300 ml (½ pint) with cold water. Leave until just beginning to set, then whisk in the yogurt. Pour into the flan case and chill until set. Remove the flan ring.

Place the cream in a piping bag fitted with a small star nozzle and pipe a lattice design over the top.

Decorate the lattice with the raspberries.

Serves 8

RASPBERRY CHEESECAKE

1 jam Swiss roll, thinly sliced
15 g (½ oz) powdered gelatine
3 tablespoons water
350 g (12 oz) redcurrants
350 g (12 oz) raspberries
50 g (2 oz) caster sugar
1 × 227 g (8 oz) carton skimmed milk soft cheese
1 × 142 ml (5 fl oz) carton single cream
TO DECORATE:
whipped cream
2 tablespoons redcurrant jelly, warmed

Line the side of an 18 cm (7 inch) base-lined cake tin or straight-sided dish with Swiss roll slices, reserving some for the top.

Put the gelatine into a cup with the water and leave to soak. Warm gently to dissolve. Reserve 125 g (4 oz) of both redcurrants and raspberries. Cook the remainder very gently for 5 minutes. Put into an electric blender or food processor and work until well blended; rub through a sieve. Stir in the dissolved gelatine and sugar until well blended.

Beat the cheese and cream together until smooth, add the fruit mixture and beat until smooth.

Pour into the prepared dish and cover with the remaining Swiss roll slices. Chill until set.

Dip the dish into hot water and invert the cheesecake onto a serving plate. Pipe a cream border around the top. Fill the centre with the reserved fruit and brush with the redcurrant glaze.

Serves 6

Mallow Raspberry Flan; Raspberry Cheesecake

STRAWBERRY CHEESECAKE

6 trifle sponge cakes, sliced
2 tablespoons orange juice
15 g (½ oz) powdered gelatine
3 tablespoons water
2 eggs, separated
150 ml (¼ pint) boiling milk
50 g (2 oz) caster sugar
2 teaspoons grated orange rind
1 × 227 g (8 oz) carton skimmed milk soft cheese
1 × 142 ml (5 fl oz) carton half cream
TO DECORATE:
50 g (2 oz) flaked almonds, toasted
300 g (10 oz) strawberries, sliced
3 tablespoons redcurrant jelly, warmed
(Picture, page 106)

Cover the base of a 20 cm (8 inch) loose-based cake tin with the sponges; sprinkle with the orange juice.

Put the gelatine into a cup with the water and leave to soak. Warm gently to dissolve. Put the egg yolks into a bowl, add the milk and stir over a pan of simmering water until thickened. Beat in the dissolved gelatine, sugar and orange rind.

Beat the cheese and cream until smooth, then stir into the custard. Whisk the egg whites until stiff, fold into the cheese mixture, then pour into the tin. Chill until set.

Transfer the cheesecake to a serving plate. Press the almonds onto the side and arrange the fruit on top. Glaze with the redcurrant jelly.

Serves 8

MICROWAVE SHORT CUTS FOR CHEESECAKES

The microwave can help in several ways when you are making uncooked and baked cheesecakes.

For easy creaming and blending, first soften refrigerator chilled cream, curd or soft cheeses in the microwave. Cook about 250 g (8 oz) cheese on MEDIUM for about 30–45 seconds.

If you plan to keep a cheesecake in the refrigerator for a couple of days, then make sure that it does not dry out by topping it with a fruity glaze. Cook 125 g (4 oz) sieved jam with 4 teaspoons water, fruit juice or liqueur on HIGH for 1–2 minutes until syrupy, stirring twice. Cool slightly, then spoon or brush over the cheesecake to coat.

Get the maximum amount of juice from citrus fruit such as lemons, limes, grapefruit and oranges by first warming them in the microwave for a few seconds. For best results, cut the fruit in half and cook on HIGH for about 30 seconds before squeezing.

GOOSEBERRY CHEESECAKE

50 g (2 oz) butter
50 g (2 oz) golden syrup
200 g (7 oz) ginger biscuits, finely crushed
500 g (1 lb) gooseberries
4 tablespoons water
75 g (3 oz) caster sugar
1 × 227 g (8 oz) carton cream cheese
300 ml (½ pint) ready-to-serve custard
1 × 150 g (5 oz) carton low-fat natural yogurt
few drops green food colouring (optional)
15 g (½ oz) powdered gelatine
3 tablespoons water
TO DECORATE:
whipped cream
gooseberries

Melt the butter and syrup, then stir in the biscuit crumbs. Press the mixture over the base of a greased 20 cm (8 inch) loose-based cake tin.

Cook the gooseberries in the water for 4 minutes, or until tender. Put into an electric blender or food processor and work until smooth. Sieve to remove pips, then stir in the sugar.

Beat the cheese until smooth, then stir in the gooseberry purée, custard and yogurt. Add food colouring, if desired.

Put the gelatine into a cup with the water and leave to soak. Warm gently to dissolve. Beat the dissolved gelatine into the gooseberry mixture.

Pour over the biscuit base and chill until set. Carefully transfer to a serving plate and decorate with piped cream and gooseberries.

Serves 8

RASPBERRY CHEESE ROULADE

5 eggs, separated
175 g (6 oz) caster sugar
2 tablespoons clear honey
75 g (3 oz) hazelnuts, finely ground

FILLING:

2 × 85 g (3 oz) packets creamery soft cheese, softened
1 × 142 ml (5 fl oz) carton single cream
2 tablespoons icing sugar (approximately)
250 g (8 oz) raspberries

Put the egg yolks and sugar into a bowl and whisk until thick and pale. Whisk the egg whites until stiff, then whisk in the honey until thick and glossy. Fold into the yolk mixture with the hazelnuts until evenly mixed. Pour into a lined and greased 33 × 23 cm (13 × 9 inch) Swiss roll tin.

Bake in a preheated moderate oven, 160°C (325°F), Gas Mark 3, for 20 to 25 minutes, until firm. Cover with a damp tea-towel and leave until cold.

Beat together the cheese, cream and 1 tablespoon sifted icing sugar and place 2 rounded tablespoons in a piping bag fitted with a small star nozzle.

Turn the roulade out onto a piece of greaseproof paper dredged with icing sugar. Cover with the remaining cheese mixture and raspberries, reserving 8 for decoration. Carefully roll up from the short edge. Place on a serving dish and decorate with the reserved cheese mixture and raspberries.

Serves 6

HIGHLAND FLAN

50 g (2 oz) self-raising flour
½ teaspoon baking powder
50 g (2 oz) caster sugar
50 g (2 oz) soft margarine
1 egg

FILLING:

1 × 142 ml (5 fl oz) carton double cream
1 tablespoon clear honey
2 tablespoons whisky
25 g (1 oz) medium oatmeal, toasted
350 g (12 oz) raspberries

Sift the flour and baking powder into a bowl. Add the sugar, margarine and egg and beat for 1 to 2 minutes, until smooth. Transfer to a lined and greased 18 cm (7 inch) fluted sponge flan tin and bake in a preheated moderate oven, 160°C (325°F), Gas Mark 3, for 15 to 20 minutes, until firm. Cool on a wire rack.

Put the cream, honey and whisky into a bowl and beat until soft peaks form, then fold in the oatmeal until evenly mixed.

Spread two-thirds of the raspberries in the flan case and cover with the cream mixture. Decorate with the remaining raspberries.

Serves 6

LEFT: *Gooseberry Cheesecake*
RIGHT: *Raspberry Cheese Roulade; Highland Flan*

INDEX

D

E

F

G

ACKNOWLEDGEMENTS

The publishers would like to thank the following individuals who were involved in the preparation of material for this book:

Photographers: Bryce Attwell, Rex Bamber, Edmund Goldspink, Melvin Grey; James Jackson; David Johnson; Roger Phillips; Charlie Stebbings; Clive Streeter; Victor Watts; Paul Williams

Photographic Stylists: Gina Carminati; Liz Hippisley; Penny Markham; Penny Misheon; Helen Payne; Marian Price; Vicky Woods

Food prepared for photography by Jackie Burrow; Carline Ellwood; Hilary Foster; Clare Gordon-Smith; Carole Handslip; Janice Murfitt; Lyn Rutherford; Jane Suthering